Praise for *VOICES*

"*VOICES* is a gift for women who are ready for positive change in their lives. Kathy Jordan provides encouragement, hope, and a different point of view for women at various stages in their lives. Kathy's talent at helping women see the greatness within themselves, and her ability to guide them gently to achieve their goals, is the basis for this book of practical tools. By capturing the voices of women in real-life scenarios, *VOICES* shows how Kathy's methods work to bring forth positive steps women can utilize to reach their present and future goals."
—CAROLE H. SULLIVAN, First Vice President, Human Resources Business Partner, Private Wealth Management, SunTrust Banks, Inc.

"Dr. Kathy Jordan has captured the many voices of women and the personal and professional journey that reflects the very essence of our pathways—who we are, what can we become, can we make a difference. Not since *In a Different Voice*, by Carol Gilligan, have we been privileged to examine the power of a woman's world through the incredibly provocative experiences that each of them has shared. It gives me hope as a woman leader, role model, mother, and colleague to know that the roads of life lead us to asking the challenging and transformative questions and letting those answers, often from the heart, guide us in our next steps. Kudos for a groundbreaking and extraordinarily insightful cacophony of voices of the lives of women."
—IRENE H. KOVALA, EdD, President, Glendale Community College

"Kathy Jordan presents a thoughtful and insightful tome that will enlighten and motivate any reader. She brings years of practical experience to the fore and does so with flair and vision. Kathy is truly a renaissance woman in every sense of the word. *VOICES* presents compelling evidence of the past, the present and the future in such a way that the reader can't help but be excited and enthused. I recommend it!"
—TOM GOODALE, Executive Director, Omicron Delta Kappa Society

"Kathy Jordan's book is chock full of insight and advice for women of all ages and at all stages in their careers and personal lives. As you move through the pages, you quickly understand that this accomplished woman is not just an expert in her field; she is also an outstanding storyteller."
—**DEBORAH L. BROWN**, Communications Consultant and former Associate Vice President for University Relations, Radford University

"*VOICES* is a tremendous resource for all women trying to navigate the waters of business and life. I highly recommend it."
—**ANNETTE COMER**, best-selling author *Rescue Me! How to Save Yourself (and Your Sanity) When Things Go Wrong*

VOICES
Words From Wise Women

Best of Luck!
Dr. Kathy Jordan

VOICES
Words From Wise Women

LEADERSHIP TOOLS for WORK and LIFE

Kathryn L. Jordan, PhD

✳ MAS PUBLISHING, LLC

MAS Publishing, LLC
Philadelphia, PA 19127
www.maspublishing.com

While the book is based on true stories, the author may have altered names and events to protect privacy or to enhance the message.

Library of Congress Control Number: 2011941042

VOICES — Words From Wise Women
Leadership Tools for Work and Life

Jordan, Kathryn L.

p. cm.
1. Business 2. Leadership 3. Career 4. Self-Help

ISBN 13: 978-0-9828128-4-6 (Softcover)

Edited by Judy Rogers • Cover design by George Foster •
Book design by Sarah Greer

Printed in the United States of America
This book is printed on acid-free paper meeting the requirements of the American Standard for Permanence of Paper for Printed Library Materials.

Dedication

To my parents,

Arthur C. Jordan and Dorothy Robertson Jordan

Their values of service to others and the potential of
everyone to achieve a dream have guided my life and
influenced this book.

Contents

Acknowledgements

I give my sincerest thanks to my family especially Bill, Jenny, Emily, Carrie, Kirsten, and to my friends and professional colleagues for believing in this project. Their encouragement motivated me to make the difficult decision to leave my position to finish this book.

I also want to thank the staff of MAS Publishing for leading me through this entire process and in particular Judy Rogers, my editor, whose excellent suggestions helped me make this book something every woman could utilize.

Thank you to all who believed in this project and were confident that these leadership and life principles needed to be available to assist others. Without you, this book would not have become a reality.

Introduction

This is a book for women and about women based on conversations with friends and clients regarding their work and life experiences. These women all wanted to find answers to one of our eternal questions, "Is there a way to achieve balance in my life roles as a woman and at the same time build a successful and satisfying career?" This book distills their experiences into general leadership principles for work and life success. You will hear the voices of real women as they speak about their lives.

The title and refrain of a popular song written by Mark D. Sanders and Tia Sillers,[1] "I Hope You Dance" captures the spirit of those conversations and the voices of the women with whom I have worked during the past twenty years.[1] Women want to "dance" and enjoy life while at the same time fulfilling the expectations of society. The lyric of the song is a woman's quiet prayer that her children find the fullness of life even in tough moments. The song struck a chord with listeners everywhere including the women in my career consulting practice.

Women struggle to balance competing demands in contemporary life. They want to find career and work satisfaction, support their families, and have a little time left over for their own interests. To help other women through the same balancing act, the women in the stories found in this book gave me permission to share their experiences. Our goal is to help others who struggle with managing the multiple roles we hold of daughter, mother, student, spouse, friend, employee, community participant, and others.

I am a career counselor and mentor. I have focused my professional practice on women and some of their unique issues in the workplace. The women with whom I worked all had different life stories or voices of experience. They used different notes or skills and utilized a range of pitches because they had unique cultural experiences, but their voices were singing in harmony. Some general themes emerged in our conversations about what it means to be a woman and build a career at the same time. All of the women wanted their lives to be satisfying and to know they had accomplished their goals. Most of them wanted to make a difference to the world and to the lives of their families.

My voice is also part of the chorus of voices you will hear in the book. I was trained as a counselor. However, I did not find my mature voice and define my specialty area to be women and their career decision-making and development, until the end of my first marriage to my college sweetheart. This experience brought forth a time of both personal and career transition. I had worked to help build his career while he was in law school. I was the mother of our two daughters, had earned two college degrees, worked part-time, and was an active volunteer in our small community. However, I now had to answer the question, "Who was I, independent of this relationship?"

During a time of personal reflection, I realized I was interested in why some people got up every day and went off happily to work while others reported to the job but had no joy in what they did. Were people a reflection of their careers? Were certain types of people attracted to particular careers or did their career paths change them? Why had some women dropped out of their careers and chosen to stay at home with their children for some period while other women did not? Did everyone really know what he or she wanted to do for a career? Why did some people change their career direction several times over the course of their lifetime and some never did find a niche?

This period of questioning ultimately led me to a lifelong interest in work and the future of the workplace. I felt my calling was to understand the process of career development and what leads to work satisfaction in order to help others. Now after years of additional study and experience, I offer my voice to those of the women who speak in this book.

As women have shared their life stories and talked about their successes, they asked additional questions. These questions were all variations on a few themes: Is there a way to find career and work success and still have a personal life? How do I find something I am passionate about doing? How do I get there? Is there a formula that will guarantee me success? Now that I have a promotion, can you help me become a great woman leader? Is there a typical leadership style associated with women?

In this book, I distill these women's voices into principles for career success and show how they can lead to a lifetime of satisfaction. Of course, every woman's definition of life satisfaction is different. However, all women talked about the importance of relationships with family and friends and how they must be integrated into their work experiences. This theme is repeated almost universally by the women's voices and at almost every age and stage of life.

Here is what I have learned. Our career includes whatever we expend effort and work to accomplish except what we do purely for pleasure. Therefore, work and career does involve both our paid and unpaid roles. Volunteer experience and work in the family setting are in fact part of our career paths. Work can occur in office settings or in unstructured situations.

Our work, like our life roles, does change over time. A career evolves as our entire lifetime of roles continues to change. As women, we emphasize different roles at different times in our lifespan—daughter, student, and friend or employee/entrepreneur, wife, mother, citizen, and community volunteer. Our careers are a mirror of our lifespan.

I found out that success is less about luck and more about hard work. The key to being successful in life almost always involves intentional acts. Finally, it has become clear that at various times in our lives dissimilar tunes or plans for work and career are appropriate. At various times, we must emphasize altered rhythms or roles.

This book is written with sincere appreciation to all the women who shared their life dreams—their aspirations with me. Together we hope to help and inspire others as they set out on this wonderful journey of work and life. We know you can find ways to celebrate and enjoy the fullness of a women's life. You can still sing, dance, succeed at work and have a balanced personal life.

—Kathy Jordan, PhD

CHAPTER ONE

KNOW YOURSELF TO FIND "PASSION"

The First Career Principle of Successful Women Is Finding Your Passion

In a "24–7 world," women play multiple roles and deal with unrelenting pressure to multi-task in each of them. Combine that with a desire to achieve or to please those who depend on us, and there is little extra time to devote to thinking about ourselves. Only a very few of us take time out to examine our lives and begin to define our goals, values, and interests. However, those of us who give ourselves a distinct time for personal reflection, find it is one of the most important things we can do to achieve life satisfaction. It is also highly correlated to career success.

I recommend that every woman set aside time, at least once every two years, to think about what is important to you and what you want to accomplish. It should be a deliberate and intentional "time out" for thinking. Solid reflection does not have to become too time consuming and can be accomplished quickly in an evening or two at home with your feet up, relaxed, and in seclusion.

THE VOICE OF LINDA, AN EXECUTIVE IN THE HEALTHCARE INDUSTRY

Women told me that taking time to reflect about their lives is a total luxury but also critical for their success. They actually make time to think about what they have achieved to date. They reflect on who they have become, and they refocus on where they want to go. We are usually just too busy to do this for ourselves!

Over ten years ago when I was working in the outplacement industry as a career coach, a women executive came into my life because her job was eliminated. Linda, a Vice President of

Marketing in the healthcare industry, told me it had been years since she had thought about why she chose to go to college or what she learned in her first job. We were reviewing her career history during an interview when she realized she had not taken any time for herself to think about her accomplishments in the last few years. She had been too busy at work to do this for her own self. She spent hours in corporate meetings thinking about corporate vision statements and developing business plans, but she had not done a business review or developed a business plan for herself. She was working day-to-day without goals for herself.

In our counseling sessions, Linda described to me how she managed to balance a marriage, the birth of a child, and the death of a parent while building her career. As a successful marketing executive, she spent hours each week focusing the public's attention on the industry products for her employer, however, her personal life and planning time were non-existent. It became a rare and very positive opportunity for this woman as she began to consider her own needs. Once Linda knew what she had already accomplished, she could set her goals for her next steps. She moved into her next position quickly after doing marketing work for herself.

The place to start a reflection process is to think about how your personality type and interests currently fit into your work and life. Solid evidence exists that people who find a good fit between their personal strengths and the requirements of a job are more successful. They love what they do. Their work utilizes their strong points and is not problematic but instead pleasurable. Working long hours or juggling tasks becomes easier.

Many women have asked me how to begin this reflection process. You will need to think about your values, interests, skills, challenges, and accomplishments. What is important to you? What do you really like to do with your time? What are you good at doing? Are there areas in your life that are a particular challenge? What are you most proud of having achieved in the past five years? You should put these ideas down on paper, as the writing will begin to make them more real, solid, and concrete. The important point is that only you can do this for yourself because no one knows you as well.

Once you have answered the previous personal questions, think about your workplace orientation and work values. I use a conceptual model based originally on the work of Edgar Schein, PhD, at the Massachusetts Institute of Technology, whose research about workplace orientations was published in the 1990s.[1] As you read the archetypes below, think about which one is a good example of whom you understand yourself to be.

For example, are you someone who seeks adventure or needs variety in the workplace? Are you motivated by the challenge of exceeding goals and expectations? If so, you may be what I call the "pirate" type personality. This is a basic and fun way to picture and understand your needs and values. If you could see yourself in an old movie storming the ship and celebrating the victory because the challenge was there, you might very well share the personality characteristics of people who excel in sports or sales and marketing careers. These people exhibit pirate-like characteristics.

In my work as I talk to people about their basic work orientations and the values on which they will build a career, I have distilled these into playful job titles to make it easy for us to understand the work values and work orientations that Dr. Schein wrote about in his book. If you are not a "pirate," perhaps you're the "gardener?" Are you the woman who finds pleasure in accomplishing a task and find it soothing and reassuring to have some predictability in your work? Do you need to know the specifics of the job process and expectations of you at work? Do you like consistent, regular feedback on your performance? Picture a gardener who understands the seasons of the planting calendar and the predictability that even after a dry spell there will be rain. The yearly rhythm of planting and harvesting provides some sense of security. Every year the gardener plants the seeds and waters them carefully, and then enjoys the harvest. Would work with structure and results give you satisfaction?

Other archetypes are:

- *"Expertise Woman"* - A woman who needs to stay current in her field. She likes to participate in continuous training and to receive recognition from her peers about her talent in meeting the challenges in the field.

- *"Girl Scout Troop Leader"* - There are other people who enjoy managing projects and people but not the direct delivery of the hands-on work. Do you like administrative work? Would you be able to motivate your scouts to canvas the neighborhoods and sell their cookies? Do you see yourself as a generalist more than a specialist?

- *"Entrepreneurial Diva"* - Do you need to express your creativity in what you do? If so, you may try to picture how one client saw herself. She called herself an idea hamster. Do you run an idea over and over in your head until you get an even better idea? Could you see yourself developing multiple business ventures?

- *"Social Activist"* - Are you motivated by a concern for society? Is it important for you to help those in need or work on behalf of a cause? Ask these questions of yourself, do I get the most satisfaction from helping others? Is my paycheck less of a motivator than helping others or my cause?

- *Independent Contractor"* - Could you see yourself working at your own pace rather than being part of a big organizational structure? Do you want to set the rules for when you work or how you get the job done? Professors reflect this career orientation and value. In their classrooms, they are in charge. Others have described working with college professors as trying to herd cats. They are an independent breed.

- *"Gymnast on a Balance Beam"* - Women with this orientation want flexibility more than anything else from their workplace. Are you a woman who is motivated toward her career but must balance her work-life with that of her personal-life? In this orientation, the hours and geographic location are critical determinants to job satisfaction.

You may see yourself strongly in one of these types or

you could be a combination of several of these orientations. I suggest you think honestly about your biggest personal needs for satisfaction in a work environment. No one type is better than another. Understanding your work orientations and personal values is one of the keys to job satisfaction. We know that your values remain fairly stable over the course of your lifetime and that it is important to find some congruence and fit between your personal values and those requirements of a job and career.

TWO WOMEN IN WORLD WAR II WHO LEFT THEIR VOICES BEHIND

Here is the story of women who did take the time to understand themselves and their world. Their messages are powerful.

Dottie and Laura were two amazing women whose lives embraced this lifelong reflection process and understanding of self. I talked to them often about their lives as I was growing up. Although one was from the West Coast and one from the Midwest, they met at a small church-affiliated college and were sorority sisters during the years immediately preceding World War II. They remained fast friends all their lives until Dottie passed away after 70 years of friendship. These women from traditional backgrounds decided in their youth that they must contribute to their world and society. This was especially clear to them after the bombing of Pearl Harbor and their graduation from college in 1941. They decided to join the military to fulfill their desire for youthful adventure and helping others. They became two of the first women naval officers during World War II. This was a huge step away from the world in which they grew up.

Dottie and Laura enlisted together, trained as officers at Smith College, and became de-coders in Washington, DC, assisting the war effort as members of the first class of Navy Waves. They were pioneers meeting a challenge that had not been taken by women before. Their lives in the post-World War II era continued to reflect an interest in assisting society as they both raised their own families and became English teachers. Well into their eighties, these two women reflected about their contributions to a generation and to society. In personality assessments, these women would have listed contributing to the "social" order as a high value. When I spoke with them, they expressed the notion that assisting others was a strong motivator, and they were able to act on this value throughout their lifetimes. Laura was a social activist all her life. Dottie was a military wife whose family was dedicated to the notion of duty and country. She believed any woman could be whatever she chose to be and encouraged women around the world with her words and actions.

It was the self-knowledge of Dottie and Laura that helped them move confidently through a time that brought amazing changes to the status of women in the workplace. In the time after World War II, traditional stereotypical notions about gender and a woman's role in society re-emerged. However, Dottie and Laura implemented the independence and confidence they found during the war experience and built careers outside of the home. They were some of the first women to balance work-life and personal-life career efforts as "pirates" and "social activists" while living in a world that expected them to be "gardeners."

After you understand your values and basic work orientation it is important to understand how your personality fits into different occupations. We know that different occupations do attract different personality types, and we know that those who play to their strengths and find a career that fits their personality are going to feel more in tune and fit better into the work environment. How well your job fits your personality is definitely related to career success. If you are interested in delving more deeply into personality and job fit, follow up with some additional reading into the theories of by Dr. Carl Jung and Dr. John Holland. There are well-known personality assessment tools associated with these authors including the Myers Briggs Personality Profile and the Holland Self Directed Search.[2] Taking a formal career assessment can help you understand yourself. It will solidify what you intuitively know from experience. A career assessment can give you additional career options or skills to explore and develop. I suggest everyone take career assessments, available online or through state employment agencies, every three to four years in conjunction with the reflection process I previously discussed.

In addition to formalized career assessments you can take, there are also many worksheets that can assist you in a process of self-discovery. At the end of this book, I have included several simple assessment tools and activity sheets that others have found helpful. The combination of career assessment instruments and self-reflection will give you a solid snapshot of your "self" at this moment in time.

Finding a passion for your career also means you must extend your understanding to the economy, the social forces, and the contemporary work environment. Once you know who you are, you will want to make wise decisions based on the future of work. Career futurists predict the job titles of the future are unknown. How we will complete the work we do will also change because technology is impacting the whole world. Those who study work insist that everyone will need to be aware of how things are changing in the workplace so we can adapt. Unfortunately, many of us do not know what other career options are available when we make a career decision.

One place to start finding the match for your values, interests, knowledge, and skills is by completing research about careers on the Internet. This tool has dramatically affected the field of career information by making critical information about specific careers available in remote geographic locations at any time of the day or night. I suggest you explore your career options by completing research on a specific job title that may interest you. What is a day in the life of a teacher, a network engineer, or a journalist really like? Or what is the demand for teachers by geographic area? What could you expect for an annual salary? The Department of Labor's Bureau of Labor Statistics[3] and its Occupational Outlook Handbook website[4] is a great place to begin to get these answers. In addition, most states have statewide employment commissions that provide free tools for self-reflection in a career search as well as information about employment options.

Once you have the basic information, you should combine the research with an interview of a person who has actually held the position. This combination approach will give you a great overview of a job's requirements. It seems simple to do, but you would be surprised how many do not take time for this research.

What holds many of us back from embracing a change of direction is that we lack the knowledge about our other career options. Not knowing how to research is common with students, but recent graduates and even alumni need to learn how to find a job related to their interests and major field of study. What can you do with a degree in English, or history, or psychology? These liberal arts areas, if combined with a minor in business and/or supported by experiences in the field or internships, can lead to a variety of options. Did you know that many of the most accomplished CEOs did not major in business as an undergraduate but rather in liberal arts?

THE DAY BEFORE GRADUATION AND THERE WAS PANIC

Here are examples about how self-knowledge and thinking about your personality and career can have a major impact.

The voice of one recent graduate: "You have got to help me, Dr. Jordan. My parents arrive this afternoon to attend our graduation tomorrow. I have trained as a pre-school teacher, and I now can't imagine myself doing this work. What should I do?" Kara arrived in my office for the first time the day before she graduated. Unfortunately, her question reveals a consistent theme I heard during the years I worked as the director of a college career center. With so much money, time, and energy invested in an educational experience it is unfortunate that many of us do not take time to measure ourselves against a job's requirements. Kara could no longer see herself working with little people most days.

In Kara's case she had done well in her studies, completed her student teaching, and worked in pre-schools and day camps over the summers to get experience in the field. However, during her senior year, as she became aware of her changing interests and needs, she felt trapped in a career before she even began. Kara could not imagine doing something she did not love for the rest of her life. We talked about her other options using her academic background and experiences. Kara left my office with a plan but she had a lot of work ahead of her to make the switch. The truth is that none of us is trapped in a single job, but we must have courage to make changes. Kara was desperately afraid of disappointing her parents as they had invested a lot of their money in the first child to go on to college.

_____

THE VOICE OF HELEN WHO GREW UP IN THE APARTHEID SOUTH

We are all different because we have unique life experiences impacted by our specific place in the world. As you begin to understand yourself, celebrate your differences, and build on them because these differences will make you valuable and successful. Helen's story is an example of how culture and your moment in history also impact the development of your career. This woman had done some deep reflection about her world and had an understanding of how race and cultural ethnicity influenced her career. She understood how the greater cultural and social backdrop against which we all develop our careers is a critical element to the career development process. Here is her story.

Helen came into my classroom several years ago to talk to my students about the impact of race on her career development. In front of the room, her statement was, "You see before you an African-American woman born into the apartheid south. My grandmother was a slave on a plantation about 15 miles from here." Helen's words stunned the students. She was an example of the importance of understanding yourself and your world, and she took that knowledge of self and used it to create a successful and satisfying career.

During the segregation era, Helen left her family and at only 14 years of age moved to Chicago to pursue both a high school and college education. Her mother had been a teacher in an African-American community. Helen's family knew that education was the way to achieve the dream of economic and social equality. In Chicago, Helen became very independent, very urbane, and she began to find her passion for economic and racial equality. During the early 1960s, her career took her into political activism in Washington, DC, and New York. She ultimately returned home to a southern small town environment to head up the restoration of a historical school for freedmen founded by the Quakers. Helen's education and career path were directly impacted by the cultural milieu and time in society during which she made her decisions. We do not build careers in isolation but in the context of the world in which we are living.

Working well into her later years, Helen continued to use self-reflection as a mechanism for staying the course with her causes even in difficult times. In her 80s, Helen was using her thinking and self-reflection time to put her life into context and to make meaning of all she had experienced. This work gave her satisfaction about her accomplishments and life story.

CHAPTER TWO

A POSITIVE SELF-CONCEPT IS ESSENTIAL

*The Second Career Principle of Many Successful Women Is
Establishing a Positive Self-Concept.*

Do you believe in yourself and project an inner confidence? A "yes" to this question is worth more than any amount of treasure—you are well on your way to building the level of self-confidence that is critical to career satisfaction. The shelves at libraries and bookstores are full of self-help titles to improve confidence levels. Be aware that building confidence and self-esteem is a process that takes time. One success will lead to another.

If you implement the self-reflection process discussed in Chapter One, it will also help you build confidence. An annual review of your career can help you recognize your previous accomplishments and skills. Employers must be able to trust that you believe in yourself. How you communicate that confidence is key to getting the big project or next promotion. Confidence can be demonstrated in many ways.

THE VOICE OF A CONFIDENT YOUNG MOTHER

Your self-concept evolves over time and is a result of accumulating experiences and how you construct meaning from these experiences. What you think to yourself—your self-talk and your interpretation of life's events and circumstances contributes heavily to your self-confidence level.

In talking to women, I have learned that many were raised with certain expectations set by their families and the cultures within which they grew up. These expectations have a powerful impact on self-esteem. We also receive messages about who we are from friends, schoolmates, as well as from society.

One summer day not too long ago, a young woman and I were discussing her previous success as a mortgage broker. She worked in the Atlanta area and established very strong relationships in her industry that lead to an exciting and profitable career. This young woman had never been able to finish college, but she was a leader in the field and never doubted herself. Her confidence was projected in her conversations, how she moved into a room, and in how she managed her personal-life.

As we talked, we also watched her two-year-old daughter practice swimming with her father at our local pool. While the mother was watching with pride, the two-year-olds' grandmother looked on in fear. I was impressed with the budding new confidence in yet a new generation in this family.

With very little encouragement from her parents, the little girl let go of the side of the pool and swam out into deep water. She never doubted and was confident that her father would catch her. Laughing she sank under the water but came back up with no doubts about her father's belief that she could learn to swim.

We continued to sit at the side of the pool and talked about this trust and confidence. The mother said that in her own life she had never once considered failure as an option because her own father always said, "Of course you can do it. You are Megan." Megan's self-esteem and confidence began early with her father's voice. Confidence began in her formative years within her family and then followed her forward into the rest of her life.

Since the housing crisis and economic downturn, Megan's career has changed dramatically. However, her inner confidence is helping her survive myriad transitions including a business bankruptcy and a divorce.

If you want to explore the impact of your family's messages on your career, you will find activity worksheets to trace your family's messages about work, life, and career at the end of this book.

_____

MENTORS HELPED ONE MEDIA EXECUTIVE BUILD
SELF-ESTEEM NECESSARY FOR CAREER SUCCESS

Other people can trace their feelings of self-worth to a teacher or mentor who believed in them while they were growing up. A very successful media relations executive I know tells the story about how she struggled in her school years for good grades never knowing she had a learning disability until much later in adulthood. This struggle was particularly difficult for her during her college years. However, there was one particular teacher who expected only her best work and who believed Joyce would reach her goals when she put forward her best efforts.

Fast forward to a recent graduation address given to the May graduates at Joyce's alma mater. The media executive addressed the parents and students and talked about the importance of believing in yourself and knowing that you can make a difference in this world. Her self-concept, though shaken because it was difficult for her to make good grades as easily as her friends, ultimately became the source of her own success. She became confident enough to leave a television career on the fast track in New York and to backpack around the world hoping to find something else she could feel "passionate" about. During her year abroad, which included working for some months at Mother Teresa's orphanage in India, this woman's self-concept grew as she recognized her own strength was in caring for others. After returning to the United States, Joyce made a difference in issues that mattered to her by becoming the media relations director at a series of high profile, non-profit organizations. Understanding herself has led to increased confidence, which has ultimately led to success.

_____

Over the years, I often wished I could wave a magic wand over my women clients. That wand would increase their self-esteem, self-confidence, and lead them to greater satisfaction with life. No, I am not the "fairy godmother," but as a career coach, I have tried to combat society's messages that force many women to limit themselves in career decisions.

Here are some of the stereotypical messages that we must combat:

• *Myth - Certain job functions are gender specific and more appropriate for women.*

Many times as I worked with a young woman in either a high school or college setting, my goal was to expand her thinking about possible career options. She had not explored some of the non-traditional career titles that were a fit for her analytical skills. Too many talented female students with great skills in the math and sciences do not persist in these subjects to become engineers, scientists, or computer programmers. Instead, they consider careers that are often held by women such as a math teacher or nurse. Is it lack of support from their families or stereotypical thinking in society that limits their career options? Staying within the traditional fields associated with women will limit salary and career options in the long-term.

• *Myth - Women are either impolite or somehow less feminine when they promote themselves or their projects.*

I believe it definitely all right to say, "I'm great at what I do" when you can substantiate your statement with facts. Believe me most of the men I have worked with are more assertive than women are in selling themselves to future employers or talking about their achievements to the boss at promotion time. I have often coached young professional women to build a portfolio of work samples and document their success for the boss because they were afraid of "bragging." A portfolio can give you more confidence during performance evaluation reviews or even in interviews.

- *Myth - Women can be hired for less since their salaries are supplemental.*

There are many women who are the sole breadwinner in their families. I have taught both young and older women to negotiate salaries by emphasizing their strengths and ability for the position. For most women, their first instinct in a job search is to accept the initial offer as final. My advice is you never will know unless you try to negotiate. Many future employees have left salary money on the table by not asking for the amount men or others are being paid for the same position. You can negotiate in every industry and at every level.

- *Myth - Effective women leaders can only lead from a feminine, softer orientation.*

There are great women leaders who are not ruled by their emotions; they make decisions based on facts, they are firm, but can also work as team builders. An example of a strong woman leader is Margaret Thatcher, Prime Minister of the United Kingdom from 1979 to 1990.[1] Her nickname became the "Iron Lady." Trained as a chemist at Oxford and then as a barrister, she led her country through war, economic recession, and great changes in the political world and her party. While Margaret Thatcher was a wife and mother, she had a reputation for taking the hard-line during an economic recession. She even survived an assassination attempt in 1984. I heard her speak at a college convocation in Virginia and came away impressed with her presence, how well read she was, and her depth of knowledge in world politics. She is the real woman leader.

Subtle messages from society have a negative impact not only on the types of work we seek, but also on how effective we can be in the job search as well. In all contemporary job searches it is critical to express confidence, and it is important to remember that a job search is partially a selling and marketing effort. You must be able to articulate your strengths to others while at the same time not implying that you can do things or achieve goals that cannot be substantiated by previous accomplishments.

A person's self-esteem truly does have a long-term impact on finding and building a career and life. To others it is not always obvious that this is an area of challenge. In fact, it is surprising which people need approval from others to bolster their self-esteem and self-confidence.

Do you remember the very sincere acceptance speech of the beautiful Sally Field when she won her 1985 academy award for *Places in the Heart?*[2] It has been quoted often because she said, "I can't deny the fact that you like me, right now, you like me." Her words spoke volumes about the importance of self-concept. She was at one of the high points of her acting career and won the Oscar. However, one of her first thoughts at the moment of triumph acknowledged that self-image could be dependent on what others thought of her. She needed external approval.

However, people who are internally focused and self-reflective are typically more satisfied with their jobs, more independent, and confident. Internally focused people typically believe they can control their own destinies through their behaviors. It is not just the acquisition of skills but the belief that you can use your skills that builds confidence.

Contrast Sally Fields' lack of confidence and dependence on what others thought of her to other women with whom I have worked and how differently they communicate about themselves. Many successful career women understand that employers and others are going to believe in them, if first they believe in themselves. They know what they can do.

I have found one way to think about your accomplishments so you can articulate these clearly to others is to utilize a Problem–Action–Result system. What *problems* have you faced at work? What *actions* did you take? What were the *results* of your work? Think through your accomplishments and write them down. Then when you look back at your work sheet, your statements are useful for writing your resumes or interviewing for a job. Thinking about your accomplishments can lead to greater self-confidence. There is also a work sheet at the end of this book that can assist you.

When you speak about your accomplishments, talk about actions and results and support your statements with examples. Bring credibility to your statements and give your listener the context. Self-knowledge and resulting confidence are critical because we live in a contemporary world framed by thousands of images of celebrities, advertisements, and peer pressure for larger salaries, bigger houses, and perfect children. You need to know what you really want instead of accepting what the world tells you to want or need. Many confident women survived and ultimately thrived because they were in touch with who they are; what they wanted; and they liked themselves for their uniqueness. Their goals were their own.

A VICE PRESIDENT SURVIVES INSTITUTIONAL CHANGE

Things will not always go your way just because you are self-confident, but if you are confident, it is possible to succeed even amidst change.

A vice president from a small private college came into my practice several years ago when her institution decided to change its historic mission from a focus on the education of young women to coed education. A shift to a coeducational experience would expand the college's number of prospective students; however, Gail, one of the vice presidents, disagreed with the decision, believing the institution would lose its unique spot in higher education. After making her case with the president and board, Gail realized her only next step would be to find another position. It was a traumatic moment to think about leaving an institution where she had invested so much of herself, but after a month of soul-searching, her confidence in her skills and accomplishments resurfaced in full measure. She submitted her resignation. I worked to have her focus on all she had accomplished to date rather than on a situation that made her angry and that she could not control.

We took some time together to really think about her goals. Did she want to stay in the same geographic location and did she want to stay in the private school arena? After clarifying her ambitions for the future, reviewing her leadership skills, and what her specific needs for institutional culture would be in the future, we developed an effective job search campaign. In less than six months Gail was back home in the Midwest closer to her family and in a position of increased responsibility.

Your level of confidence also manifests itself in how you will perform a job. I have observed a variety of women who had a chance to take on a new leadership role. A pattern soon emerged. Women who are more confident in their own accomplishments and strengths tend to make decisions based on open communication channels seeking input from throughout the organization. These women seek out diversity and listen to all opinions. They are not afraid to hear different points of view from their peers.

Most self-confident women were likely to use teamwork strategies. These women leaders also had the following attributes:

- They did not feel threatened by other ideas but rather drew on the strengths of many and then made their own decisions.
- They could delegate and let others on the team accept some of the accolades for a job well done.
- They did not micro-manage the project and expected others on the team to be able to accomplish the tasks at hand.
- These women did not look back or second-guess themselves.

In part, they had the skills necessary for success in today's business world that requires decisiveness and teamwork combined.

CHAPTER THREE

PARTICIPATE IN CONTINUOUS LEARNING

The Third Principle for Success Is Participation in Continuous Learning

Try to learn something new every day. This is the mantra of the future. Even the ancient Greeks knew that continuously learning and the consideration of new ideas was essential, "If a man neglects education he walks lame to the end of his life." (Plato 428 BC – 348 BC)[1]

Since the World War era, the United States' commitment to financial support for educational pursuits has enabled many to expand their learning. Our democratic traditions have encouraged both men and women to believe education is a key to success. Going to high school, getting a college degree, or learning a new skill in the crafts and trades provided access to the American Dream and achievement of economic prosperity in our equal pursuit of goals.

Fast forward to the contemporary workplace and futurist predictions about the nature of work, and the ancient truth of Plato is even more valid today. The Hudson Institute's study for the Department of Labor on the future of the United States workplace (*Workforce 2020*)[2] told us that we would be competing in a global economy and that our workforce would become much more diverse by race, gender, and age.

The report also predicts that the ways we do our work would change with the growing influence of technology. New job titles would become necessary as we found new ways of completing tasks, and all of those working would need new skills. We have moved from the manufacturing society to the information exchange and service-based economy.

This means that every woman who wants to remain current in the workforce will need to frequently evaluate her skills;

calculate the demand for her work; and always be looking for additional training. Statistics from the U.S. Department of Education show that the more education an individual achieves the more salary and social mobility can be expected over the course of a lifetime.[3] This relates not only to obtaining formal degrees but also to short-term learning options on the job or in certificate programs. Learning broadens your career perspectives and beliefs.

Access to education, which accommodates our busy life styles as women, is available by distance-learning technologies and computer-based options everywhere and at any time. Learning can be self-paced or in-class and available for any topic from personal development, such as acquiring leadership or financial management skills, to technical training. There is no reason not to keep pace with changes or to look for ways to improve on-the-job skills. However, many people choose not to keep up.

THE VOICE OF A WOMAN RESISTING CHANGE

In speaking with people who have either lost their job or been passed over for a promotion, it is apparent that some have chosen not to continue to learn. A voice of one woman spoke for many clients when she said, "I just have five more years until retirement and I really do not like school. I just can't face returning to the community college. I should not have to do this!" In her worldview, she did not want to change, move forward, and sadly in a rapidly changing workplace she was not going to achieve additional success or quite possibly, she might even lose her job.

She gave up trying to adapt to the technological changes at work, and she just wanted to hang on until retirement. I lost track of her but have often wondered what happened to her during that last five years? Did she have the money she needed in retirement to sustain her needs? Was she able to hang on to that job? Did she return to work in another field but at a lower income level?

<hr/>

CONTRAST THAT TO THE VOICE OF KARLY
AS SHE RETURNED TO SCHOOL AT AGE 50

"Quirky, beautiful, and a grandmother at 50, Karly was a beautician in a small town, and asked me to write a reference for her to the community college. She was competing for a scholarship funded by a women's business sorority that supports non-traditional women returning to school. After years in a long-term but rocky relationship that finally disintegrated, Karly needed to find another way to earn her living. A previous injury made it impossible to work full-time in a job that required her to stand long hours. Her goal was to become financially independent so could leave the abusive relationship. It is interesting that for many, a return to education is highly correlated to a dramatic change in personal lives. After two years of working part-time and going to school full-time, Karly received an associate degree in business with a focus on the legal field. She was able to find a position in the business side of a grocery chain that provided a regular income and benefits. However, it was a long road and many times Karly talked about quitting. She started her transformation without knowing how to use a computer and that was just step one on the long road to independence.

In a proactive career management mode if you appraise your skills and know that they are in demand, you are on the right track. However to keep working, given the rate of change, it may still mean that you will need to refine or add to your skills every few years.

For example, in manufacturing environments, computers have taken over some of the tasks; learning to use the new software programs and embracing the changes has been critical if you wanted to retain a job.

Once you know you must continue to pursue education, it is also extremely important to understand your own preferences for learning. You can adjust your options to your learning style so you actually enjoy the process of learning new ideas. Some of us learn better through hands-on experience; some need a mentor, coach, or teacher to assist us in the learning; and some like to learn by reading, writing, and passing the competency tests on their own. There is no single best way to learn. The critical thing is to have the desire.

MEET SALLY WHO STAYS ON THE CUTTING EDGE

I met a senior banker responsible for executive recruitment in Richmond, Virginia, and enjoyed watching as her career developed. Sally has remained continually employed and been promoted to a six-figure salary when many others in banking have not been as fortunate. She disclosed to me that she had never finished her college education and as a single woman felt it was impossible financially for her to leave work and return to school. Instead of feeling vulnerable in a rapidly changing industry, she has taken advantage of every learning opportunity offered to her over the 25 years of her career.

This contributed in large measure to her continuing rise through the profession. She started in sales with an extroverted personality and a professional demeanor, was promoted into human resources and executive recruitment, then into organizational development and training initiatives. She now works in executive coaching situations in the corporate headquarters of a mega bank. In addition to corporate on-the-job training, this woman has also been a strong advocate for learning in her off hours. She listens to tapes on topics of interest, attends conferences of her own choosing, and generally is always developing and moving forward.

A WOMAN MILITARY OFFICER WHO BUILT A SECOND CAREER

What would you do if you finished an Army career in the military police and were only in your early forties? Would you retire and play golf for the next 40 years of your expected lifetime? One woman told me about retiring from active duty, getting married for the first time to another military retiree, and then both of them deciding to pursue their master and doctoral degrees. This woman now works on a college campus and loves her second career. Because of her military experience, she has financial independence and that has put her in a unique position as the politics at her institution play out around her. She has the luxury of only staying in her position as long she wants and not because she must. Her success is attributed to being proactive and deciding to seek re-training. As with so many others, her decision to pursue additional training was accompanied by a personal transition and lifestyle change.

In fact, the U.S. Department of Labor[4] predicts that many of us will retire and then go back to work as consultants, part-time employees, or in entrepreneurial options. If this is the future, then your career (what you intentionally spend effort at achieving) and learning are not over at any age. You will continue to evolve and will also need new skills and ideas.

Use the following process to begin organizing your future education and training options:

- Establish short-term and long-term goals for yourself
- Begin to attain your goals through targeted behaviors and an action plan
- Self-monitor your progress toward the goals through use of a journal/calendar
- Evaluate your plan and adapt to next cycle

See the worksheets for career action planning at the end of this book.

CHAPTER FOUR

FIND JOY IN CHANGE

The Fourth Career Principle Is Finding Joy in New Challenges

If you are concerned about employability or advancing in your field, it is critical to become the flexible person who not only likes variety but also can embrace change. Successful women I have coached understand this fourth principle. They have learned to put anxiety behind them and accept this 21st century reality. In the restructured workplace there is no guarantee of a life-long job, and as we've discussed, up-to-date skills, self-direction, and finding the joy in new challenges are critical to success. Is it possible to find a balance between wanting things to stay the same and yet keep up with changes in the world?

VOICE OF A RETIRED BUT "NOT RETIRING" WOMAN

Our conversation took place about three years ago at a retirement celebration. "So you taught school for 20 years and had three husbands, what are you planning at age 65?" Her answer was she wanted to find new activities to bring structure and purpose to her life. "I need to find something new to keep me vital and engaged with the world." We began discussing second career options. As we talked, she described an already happy full life. She was thinking of finding a part-time job as she still had lots of energy, and she could not see herself without a daily goal. She knew she was not done and had more to contribute to society.

Margaret lives with her husband, a retired librarian, and interacts weekly with her three sons and three grandchildren of whom she is immensely proud. She just retired after a long career as an English teacher, gifted coordinator, and technology director in public and private schools. Like all of us, she also had her own share of heartaches including several marriages and a father from whom she was estranged. However, at 65 years of age Margaret was just beginning to explore the next steps in life. She was excited to see what could come next.

We talked about following her life-long love of fine jewelry and how she could utilize that passion to find a second career option. She had previous experience in sales and strong personal relationships in her region that she maintained during 30 years of friendships. How could she combine this interest in people and jewelry into something that would provide a supplemental income so she and her husband could travel or buy some of the extras she wanted in retirement?

Ultimately, she decided to learn the jewelry trade by working in an upscale new jewelry store in a town about thirty minutes away. This provided her on-the-job training in gemology and exposure to the world of jewelry sales. Imagine her excitement when she got a chance to travel to Las Vegas and a jeweler's convention to assist with the buying for the store.

Margaret is an excellent example of a woman who in retirement found a paid, outside activity that let her "play and work" in a new job. Instead of staying with everything she knew in education, Margaret embraced change and found a great second career. She utilizes her skills honed in teaching when she helps others find a piece of jewelry to purchase. She explains the benefits of each piece when asked, listens to the customer's needs, and then assists them to find the best fit. It's a relationship-based sales approach. Her extroverted personality and strong communication skills have served her well. She knows how to handle both pleasant and difficult customers just like she effectively dealt with a variety of students, parents, and teachers in her first career. Eventually, this woman would like to own a business selling estate jewelry online and to those with whom she has already established a reputation of trust and confidentiality.

When you think about leaving one career, it always presents an opportunity to embrace change and move on to another exciting new segment of life. The choice is yours.

Successful men and women have acknowledged that the rate of change in our world has accelerated, driven by the pace of technological advances. It is the people who can adapt to new ways of work that will survive. However, this is not a new idea. Charles Darwin wrote, "It is not the strongest of the species that survives or the most intelligent, but the one most responsive to change."[1] Now years later, Darwin's words are truer than ever.

Developing an eagerness to seek out the newest strategy or try the newest technological gadget is not natural to every personality type, especially those who enjoy security and put a high value on knowing expectations of the job or having stability in life. In fact, psychologists tell us that most human beings like the status quo and resist change. Workers must have a strong sense of identity and resilience to cope with change.

We may have difficulty with change because of our social context. These barriers may be related to gender, financial constraints/needs, the ability to control or impact the change, or disadvantages associated with occupying a position in society like age or race. Also, some people may have mental health issues and negative belief systems. How many of us know someone who holds a negative view about what they can accomplish and talk themselves into believing they cannot change?

Because change is a fact of contemporary life, it is important for us to learn how to manage the stress of change and turn the tension that change creates within us to a positive. Change management is a field that has produced some significant writing including the work of William Bridges in his book, *Transitions: Making Sense of Life's Changes*.[2] We understand "change" is that which is external to us while the word "transition" is used to understand how we change within ourselves and adjust to change.

Bridge's stages of adjustment to change can help us handle the transition process we go through when experiencing both expected and unexpected changes. One of the rules he states is,

"Every transition begins with an ending. We have to let go of the old thing before we can pick up the new—not just outwardly, but inwardly, where we keep our connections to the people and places that act as definitions of who we are." We must recognize that in a change cycle there are endings and we stop the old way of doing things. This is followed by a neutral zone where we can explore options. Then comes a time of new beginnings and we can anticipate some of our internal adjustments.

The most successful women I know understand change is inevitable and acknowledge that some of life's changes will be difficult. They choose to see change as positive. To handle difficult changes, they use their healthy stress management techniques and leverage their strong self-esteem. This is especially true when a change occurs that taps into our core values or belief system.

MEET MS. PATEL ON HER JOURNEY BETWEEN TWO CULTURES

Many believe the third wave of globalism in the workplace will be a talent wave. This means that you will be working with people from around the world in different time zones and adapting to new cultures. It is not just personal changes or our arrival at a new life stage that will force us to embrace change. It is also the competition in our global, free market. It puts pressure on all of us to adapt if we want to remain employed.

For example, someone living abroad may be able to complete a work assignment here in the United States because employers and employees are no longer bound by geographic location. It's the person who is able to complete the task or project in the most cost effective and efficient manner that ultimately will have the job. Sometimes that means leaving your comfort zone of familiar places and people.

I'd like to introduce Ms. Patel, a woman whose life and career during the past ten years is a lesson about learning to embrace change. Our relationship began with a telephone call to New Delhi, India. I called her for an interview for a graduate assistantship. I have often wondered what might have happened, if I had not placed that call because the change cycle it began was unexpected. Ms. Patel's decision to accept the graduate assistantship and travel to the United States to earn a master's degree in corporate and professional communications set in motion a chain reaction that moved her into immersion in another culture.

The person I interviewed during the telephone call was a young, recently married, and highly intelligent young Indian woman who had worked in journalism perfecting her English language skills. She knew she would be making some large external changes including leaving her mother, father, and husband behind in India while studying abroad. This was huge as her family was a very important part of her life. Both of her parents were business professionals in India, and as their only daughter, they wanted Ms. Patel to be all that she could become. She and her husband hoped that ultimately he would join her in a graduate program the following semester.

When we first met in person, Ms. Patel had arrived late the evening before to begin a new stage of life in a small southern college town. Knowing no one and with no support from the university, she had spent her first night sleeping on the floor of an empty new apartment. I knew then I had met a risk taker. Different foods and customs as well as new clothes, teachers, friends, and a graduate assistantship were all part of her first weeks. Her internal transitions were huge and largely unanticipated. She was lonely and devastated when, after the first few months, it became apparent her husband would be unable to secure admission to graduate school in the U.S. This led to their long separation and eventually a divorce.

Her parents with a different cultural reality had difficulty accepting her choice to remain in the U.S. without her husband and this in turn had ramifications in their own marriage in India. Ms. Patel became estranged from her family for several years.

Stress from coping with change was Ms. Patel's constant companion as she pushed forward through these difficulties and earned her degree. She found work in her field and built a new life. However rough it was, she always projected a cheerful positive attitude. She changed her expectations.

Instead of thinking she wanted to work in the high tech California Silicon Valley, Ms. Patel decided she wanted an internship with a small technology firm near her university. After working hard and offered a full-time position with this firm, she ultimately moved to Washington, DC, and made a very successful career.

Ms. Patel is a model of a woman who adapted to new career goals, new lifetime role expectations, and even some of her most basic needs related to eating and dressing had slowly changed. Her life story illustrates how important it is to know what you want and be able to adapt to a changing environment by using a positive frame to see the changes. Part of the strategies that made Ms. Patel successful in her adaptations included the ability to rebuild a social structure with new friendships with other international students and her American co-workers here in the United States.

Despite being a fairly private person, she learned she could talk over her life changes and could ask for help. She learned to drive a car by borrowing an old car from her roommate who took her to get a learner's permit. A woman she met during her graduate assistantship helped her co-sign for her first apartment after graduation since she had no financial track record in the U.S. She saved her money from the job, bought a car and traveled to visit other family members living in the United States.

Some of our personal stress related to change can be diffused by our confidence in our own abilities and performance combined with a strong sense of self-knowledge. These can give you a sense of security in the workplace and also let you become part of the "free agent nation."

There are activities at the end of this book to help you move into proactive career management and prepare you to participate in a radically changing employment world.

CHAPTER FIVE

KNOW YOUR DEMAND AND SALARY POTENTIAL

The Fifth Career Principle Is Knowing How to Negotiate Your Worth

A woman leader I know recently learned that she was paid one third less than the men who occupied the same role within her large organization. When she received her promotion and assumed additional responsibilities, the amount of raise assigned to her promotion was determined by her male boss based on a subjective decision. Now carrying more responsibility than all the others at the same level, this woman was behind on salary and had lost both the faith and motivation to continue growing her area. She was silently angry.

It is hard to believe in our society, built on principles of equality, that this type of salary discrimination continues between men and women for equal work. However, government statistics on annual salaries confirm this difference still exists in the pay ranges between men and women. This continues years after women have assumed full-time work roles and have equal experience. While our society bears responsibility for this discrimination, it is also our individual responsibility to help so all women receive equal pay for equal work. We have to lobby on our own behalf for an equal salary and have the confidence to do it.

Could you answer these questions with specific data? Do you know your earning potential in your field? What your salary potential is in the next state, across the country, or abroad? Are you employable in another industry? Do you know what other employers seek people with your skills?

Most of the women I've worked with do not negotiate salary at the time of a job offer, and many cannot answer the questions above. In fact, about 90% of my women clients, regardless of age, do not think about negotiation strategy as part of the job search process. This unwillingness to negotiate and ask for more continues to keep women behind from the moment they begin their work responsibilities. I have observed that there are distinct gender differences in thinking about salary. Most of my men clients talk about salary as one of the first topics mentioned in any employment conversation, while most women begin a work discussion about location or interests and the discussion about salary comes up later.

A RECENT GRADUATE NEGOTIATES HER FIRST SALARY OFFER

We've discussed that many women do not keep close tabs on their own careers because they're too busy taking care of business for others. We leave our own careers unattended until forced to consider another job option due to circumstances. We also know that sometimes, due to a lack of experience or because of their social position and cultural norms, women place constraints on their salary expectations and career choices.

However, it turns out many of the most successful women are always prepared to take advantage of the unplanned happenstance or an unexpected job opportunity. One reason is they pay close attention to their earning potential. They understand their "value" or salary potential and the demand for their skills in the marketplace. They're prepared when that next great option arrives.

About two years ago when college graduates were struggling to find a first career option in a down economy, I got a telephone call from a young woman who was graduating with a degree in social work. She had applied for a case manager position at the agency where she had done her internship and the interview had gone well. She received an offer but was disappointed in the salary as it was at the bottom level of the range that was advertised. "I told them I was happy they wanted to hire me, but I needed some time to think it over. What should I do? Should I take the job even though it will be difficult for me to live in this area on the amount they offered? I know they are paying others at this agency more. Can someone in social work negotiate a higher salary?"

This graduate was already ahead of many because she had done the research and knew the national average for beginning social workers, plus she had done personal interviews with others within the agency and knew their salary ranges. Before she called the organization back with a reply, we developed a negotiation strategy that would emphasize her fit for the organization and her enthusiasm for the job. We wanted her to reemphasize why she was the best candidate for the position before she asked for an increase in the initial salary offer.

After the initial comments, she planned to say, "I know that some others have started out at the lowest level of the salary range for this position. However, because of my previous experience during my year-long internship with this organization and the excellent reviews I received, I would like to be considered at the second step of entry level pay range." She was in a strong negotiating position because she had already established a great reputation by working with the clients and other staff, and she had received a wonderful final evaluation of her work.

As we talked about negotiation strategy, she made a decision that if they would not make a slightly higher initial offer to recognize her as a recent graduate with one year of experience, she would look elsewhere. She knew the value of her experience. She had other options that helped her negotiate from a position of strength. Her knowledge of the system and skills gave her confidence to negotiate a higher starting salary. She was not willing to accept a starting salary that didn't acknowledge her previous experience and demonstrated skills.

In negotiations, only you can evaluate your need for the job versus your need to be paid a higher salary. This young graduate's decision to negotiate to begin at a higher initial salary would have impact on her future cost of living raises. While not everyone is in this position during negotiations, I know that many times women leave money on the table because they do not try to negotiate. An employer can say there is no additional room to increase the pay but if you do not try to negotiate for the best salary possible, you will not get the money.

Here's how you can get started. Look at other job possibilities and know first if they are a fit for your goals and skill sets. Know whether this job possibility would be a good financial move for you. Be prepared to stay ahead of the competition by responding quickly to any opportunity as soon as you hear about it.

Always be able to:
- Find ways to network within the organization
- Keep your resume current and up-to-date with your latest accomplishments
- Articulate your "fit" with previous experience and skills
- Know how much salary you can command in the marketplace

The U.S. Department of Labor's *Occupational Outlook Handbook*[1] posts national averages and median salaries in most career fields. It is important to know this information by city, state and region. There can be a significant difference in salary based on the cost of living differentials across the country. The Internet has a variety of sites that can make salary calculations based on location and job classification. You should use these tools whenever you are considering a job move.

In addition to understanding salary differences by location, it is critical to understand how your skills may be utilized in a variety of industries and in different job functions, if you are truly going to manage your career in a proactive manner. Each of us has a job function or set of tasks that we do and an industry in which we complete these tasks. For example, you may be a police officer (job function) for a city government (industry location) or an English teacher (job function) in a high school setting (industry location.) If you understand how your skills can be valuable either in a totally different work setting, or in another that's similar, or just slightly different from your current situation, it can be a great advantage. This knowledge gives you the power to expand your employment options and build your salary potential as you move forward in your career.

The easiest career transition to make and assign a salary level is when you choose the same job function in the same industry in which you currently work. For example, you move from a teaching position in one school district to another. Alternatively, you might move from teaching in a rural school system to an urban school system in your state. In each of these cases, you simply factor in the geographic differences in salaries and evaluate the option.

However, what if you're the English teacher in a rural high school and you want to do something totally different in a new urban location? Would you know what other organizations or companies are likely to hire someone with a teaching background and an excellent command of the English language?

Perhaps the most effective ways for you to get this type of information is by talking to others in your field. They will know what other work options colleagues have turned to when they left the field. Never underestimate the power of networking. It is the source of great information, and is related to your abilities to develop relationships. If you like people and enjoy talking to others, then use networking extensively. Conversations with peers in your field are invaluable. Much has been written recently about the importance of relationships in an increasingly high tech world. Social networking sites have made it possible for you to identify colleagues around the globe. These people are an invaluable tool in career management and job search strategies. While I never suggest asking about specific salaries from a networking contact, you may ask open-ended questions about others in the field and their salary ranges to gather needed information.

Another great way to acquire information about salary levels, as well as understand demand, is to read job descriptions when they are posted as employment advertisements. Analyze these job descriptions to determine how your skills match the requirements of the positions. What salary levels are associated with levels of education, number of years of experience, and skill sets? I usually suggest you read the Sunday classifieds, either online or in the newspaper, from beginning to end over a period of several weeks. You will begin to see some patterns. How many job advertisements do you see for people with your education, experience level, and skills? This will help you understand value based on demand. You may have great skills but if there are no related advertisements, it highlights lack of demand.

Employers usually seek to hire those individuals who have previous experience in their field as well as specific skill sets. To clearly highlight the match between your qualifications and their requirements, you will need to demonstrate the match point-by-point—employer requirement and your accomplishment. Show the employer what you know and have accomplished in the past is very similar to what they are seeking.

For example, the classroom teacher was in a job function that is like the trainers who work in a business or industry setting. She could demonstrate curriculum development, instructional design, student evaluations, etc., with one population and extrapolate from the classroom situation to a business training setting.

If you understand how your skills and experience translate across industry settings and know the current salaries in the field, you may want to make a transition. Remember this—if you do choose to change job functions or industries, you may take a step backward in salary for a few years until the transition is complete. In other words, this may mean taking a pay cut for two to three years before your salary catches up to its previous level.

However, it is by knowing how to transition your employment across industries and functional areas that provides you with the most options. Ultimately, you will have more control over employment and usually greater value in the workplace. A career that is managed across industries illustrates the person is flexible, adaptable, and can handle a degree of risk to achieve personal goals.

In other economic times, this type of career management may have been perceived as reflective of someone who did not know exactly what they wanted to accomplish. However, in the last 20 years, the proactive career manager is the person who has remained employed and intellectually engaged in the work-life.

Here is a way to organize your thinking about demand and salary across industries:

- Compare job postings you find by how closely related they are to your current job function and industry classification.
- Remember those jobs most closely related to your current situation are the easiest to achieve in the short-term, but may become a career stopper long-term.
- It is important for you to run this analysis every few years. In pro-active career management, you want to make career choices rationally and consider all options.

VICE PRESIDENT MAKES A SMOOTH TRANSITION TO A NEW INDUSTRY

A former client had worked for nearly 20 years at the same location rising to a vice presidency with significant responsibilities and a great salary. When a dramatic change occurred in the executive suite, this woman was given six months' notice that her contract would not be renewed. As you may know, this story is all too familiar in the realities of a rapidly evolving and economically stressed global work environment.

Many people in such a scenario become immobilized by shock or anger and let several months elapse before they begin to plan a career transition. This was not the case with my client. She chose to quietly prepare herself for the end of her current job by beginning to implement a plan she had already developed for a consulting practice and her next possible career step. As in the past, she was prepared to manage herself successfully in case a change occurred in her work environment.

This woman wanted an entrepreneurial option that would give her the control and flexibility to pursue specific types of work after so many years of working for others. Almost immediately after she was notified, this woman began to establish a public relations consulting firm. By the time she exited the vice president's role, she knew her business philosophy, had developed her business plan, and researched the scope of her market. During her last six months, she had established networking contacts to seek advice on consulting in her industry and had several clients waiting in line for consulting work.

Entrepreneurial options, as the one described, are frequently mid-way points between major career shifts. They can help a person understand their specific marketable skills; the value of these skills to another organization; and the demand for their work. More women are taking entrepreneurial options than ever before, and we know most new job creation begins with a crisis that becomes an opportunity.

CHAPTER SIX

BUILD YOUR LEADERSHIP SKILLS

*The Sixth Career Principle Is to Self-Develop Leadership
Skills to Ensure Competitiveness*

Most of us have met individuals during our lifetime that inspired us with their performances as leaders or managers. How would you describe these people? The leader who inspired you may have been someone you met at work, or while you volunteered at local food bank. Perhaps, it's a family friend or someone you met at school. As more women have accumulated significant experiences, many have asked me, "How can I become a leader in my organization? Are there some characteristics that all great leaders share?"

Think about it. You may have been impressed with a personal characteristic, a thinking and decision-making style, or how a person interacted with others. The role model for your future leadership skills is the person that you thought to yourself, *I would like to try to be more like him/her when I have a chance to manage or lead.* Role models are critical in teaching us about ourselves; they show us examples of who we want to become. Successful women, who are satisfied with their careers, usually speak about their observations of others. They have learned from previous experience and everyday events, and are ready to apply what they have observed when given a chance for leadership.

Are women leaders born or made? Through the years, there has been considerable discussion in the literature and research as to whether leaders are born or taught leadership characteristics. The best recent research leads us to the answer—"that leaders are mostly made." (Ronald E. Riggio, PhD, *Psychology Today*, March 2009)[1]

We know there are some basic personality characteristics associated with obtaining a leadership role and being an effective leader.

These include:
- Extroversion and communication, as the leader must convince others to follow
- A degree of boldness or assertiveness
- Some degree of comfort with risk-taking
- Intelligence, especially the social intelligence to perceive social solutions
- Empathy to understand what others think and need, so they will follow the leader

All these characteristics are associated with leadership. Today there is also a realization in the field of leadership development that it is possible for us to self-develop our leadership capacities. This is great news for women as they build careers.

Currently women are rising to leadership positions not only in big businesses but also in government, education, the service industries, and in entrepreneurial opportunities. Women now comprise nearly half of the managerial workforce with 49% of managerial and professional specialty positions. We know 60% of all marriages are dual-earner marriages, and women were more than 50% of the corporate workforce in the year 2000 according to Department of Labor Statistics.[2]

Still disparity remains. Three principal factors seem to contribute to the perpetuation of the "Glass Ceiling" barrier. They include recruitment practices, lack of opportunity to participate in corporate leadership development tracks, and the lack of shared sense of responsibility for equal employment opportunity. However, you can begin to hear the sound of the glass ceiling just beginning to shatter, and there is now more discussion about the new "feminine leadership style." What do you think? Do women prefer a particular leadership style? If we know that many women do not get a chance to participate in employer-sponsored leadership development training, are there courses or activities women can pursue that will help develop skills to become a leader or manager when the opportunity arrives?

The truth is that all of us can become better at leading and managing others by building on what we have observed and understanding why it worked for others. We should analyze what was effective and meaningful to us, and then adapt it to our own personality types. The number one rule is to be authentic to yourself but incorporate other models into your thinking. Women must find the leadership style that best suits their values and personality and an organization that is open to their style of leadership.

The great women leaders I have met think about finding the fit between the requirements of the environment, their personality type, and leadership preferences. They are intentional about when, how, and where they lead. Different types of leadership styles are required in different settings.

To understand these differences, just think about the type of leaders who are successful in a military-type environment compared to leaders who successful in a public school system. Visualize a general like George Patton or the superintendent in your local school system.

These two work environments are dramatically different and the environmental factors require particular personality characteristics of a leader in each environment. It is important to recognize leadership styles that are effective in the two very different settings. The military work environment is about "command and control." The effective leader in this environment needs to work through hierarchical levels of the system and be directive. Such a leader must get things done with lightning speed. Subordinates must follow direction without questioning motives, and often, total secrecy is required.

The school system environment is more about consensus building, particularly since teachers are somewhat independent in their own classroom, and there are many constituencies to consider, often with competing agendas. In this example, there must be joint goal setting and action planning since implementation will require each teacher's buy-in. The leader's goal is to have each teacher cover the same content material to ensure student learning and achievements meet the standards of learning.

Neither environment is better. They are equally effective at completing different types of work. It's just they are dissimilar.

_____

MEET PATRICIA, A POSITIVE WOMAN LEADER, ROLE MODEL AND MENTOR

I first met Pat during the time I returned to earn my doctorate. She quickly became a boss, mentor, role model, and friend. By the time we worked together, Pat had earned a major academic leadership role on a large university campus. She was married to a college engineering professor, and her career was a major focus in life. Her professional goal was to increase the number of women in leadership roles in higher education, and to make the academic world less "chilly" and more accepting of the unique needs of women who want to build careers and work in higher education.

As I watched and worked with this colleague, I was continually amazed at her ongoing focus toward her goal and her leadership style. In both her personal and professional life, she concentrated on mentoring and developing other women. She was able to lead and manage with decisiveness, deliver effective execution of her action plans, and mobilize women with different personalities and needs to achieve her purposes. Pat's personal style was inclusivity for all and was known for her tact, humor, common sense, and emotionally intelligent approaches. She was rewarded for her work by a succession of chief executives.

The only time I ever saw this woman waiver, during our 20-year professional association, was in her leadership of a project team for a major institutional grant concerning women in the sciences. Two women faculty members on the team held very different views of how to move the team and project forward. This was the first time she had experienced such a level of intra-team conflict that threatened to derail the project as a whole. It was even more distressing to her since it was a team of women working on issues critical to women faculty. The project goals were more important to her than carrying the title or role as leader of the team. She gave up the leadership role so the groups could continue productively, with less personal conflict. While this was a painful lesson in group dynamics, her self-knowledge, wisdom, and personal self-esteem did not let an incident derail the ultimate success of the work. She put things into perspective and moved forward.

Recently, I stood in the back of a room and listened to the accolades for her work during a retirement reception for Pat. I thought again about the model she had set for other women in the state. It was wonderful to see how far reaching her impact had been in the world of education. By truly focusing on others, she had found immense personal and career satisfaction. It was a career well spent. In talking with her later about what comes next, she explained that retirement means the transfer of her energies to other issues in the non-profit world that impact the lives of women. How remarkable.

Discussion in the literature centers on how women display leadership characteristics that are "transformational." Women are consensus builders playing the role of teacher or coach, and generally described as mentors and motivators of employees. The truth emerging from much of the recent work is that some women do assume a leadership style that is very much in step with the team-oriented and project management workplaces found in the contemporary business world. The timing could not be better for the women who lead by this style. However, not all women do. Keep in mind that leadership style is more about personality, previous role models, and societal expectations than just about gender.

Whatever your style, recognize when an organization may be ready for your leadership style and when it is not. In World War II, Winston Churchill's effective leadership led the United Kingdom and Allies to victory, but his style was not acceptable after the war years being voted out of office after he helped secure the victory. What worked in a time of war did not set well with Britain in a time of peace. History teaches us about timing. A leadership style can be effective at different times in society as well as at different times in a lifespan.

As with some of the earlier comments in this book, I have found it critical to understand who you are if you're to become an effective leader. You must believe in your own style and be grounded in your strengths, weaknesses, and the values that drive your actions. You can develop your own leadership style and be ready when the leadership moment arrives.

One characteristic of all excellent leadership is strong communication. To be effective, you must be able to communicate your vision and goals in a 360° perspective throughout the organization. It is critical that everyone who works with you, including those to whom you report and those you direct, are kept knowledgeable about the project you are leading. Managing the information flow either upward or across organizational boundaries is an area where some leaders may fail. They take action without involving others who may have a critical stake in the outcome or by not keeping them up-to-date. This was the case with the next example.

NON-PROFIT CEO LEADS HER ORGANIZATION TO LOW MORALE AND LOWER MARKET SHARE

It is an example of the perfect storm. Have you wondered what would happen if an inexperienced leader, who was selected through a heavily influenced political process, took over an organization just as the economy was in a crisis situation? This happened five years ago and the results hold many lessons for other emerging leaders. A new woman leader was selected for a prestigious Chief Executive Officer position based on the political and persuasive powers of one of the Board of Directors. The organization wanted her to succeed as their first female CEO, especially since serving women clients had been the initial mission. However, within months this executive demonstrated poor communication skills and an authoritarian style that took the organization to new all-time low outputs. Client numbers were down and donations fell off dramatically.

Leadership is always critical, but especially when economic times are tough. Within months of her arrival, this woman had to make some difficult and critical decisions to move a large organization forward in a time of declining revenues. She did so in a unilateral and authoritarian manner. She made a number of high profile personnel changes, abruptly and seemingly capriciously dismissing long-time managers and bringing in outsiders without any significant experience in that type of nonprofit organization. Her actions created a climate of fear among employees and concern for the future of the organization. She gave the appearance of listening to groups of people from both outside and within the organization as she began to put together a five-year plan of goals. However, it slowly became clear to many that there were predetermined agendas at work, and she had not communicated honestly with staff, clients, and stakeholders.

Within six months, it was apparent that no decision could be made at any level in the organization without her final authority and workflow slowed to a standstill. It was hard to get things done. Staff either feared moving forward with any new initiative or had to wait for her approval. Could an experienced leader and a confident leader have communicated her agenda and motivated the organization to change?

As events played out, she lost credibility with many on her leadership team and throughout the organization. A public crisis played out in the news when a popular employee was dismissed with virtually no notice and scant rationale. She apologized to the community and explained that she had observed her leadership style in others and believed that it was needed to be successful. She committed to stronger communication channels but went forward in the previous authoritarian style. I believe she wanted to change but could not.

Her communication style was to listen to an inner circle and make decisions without the benefit of organizational history and understanding of the reasons for many previous decisions. She invited others to talk to her but in carefully managed appointments. An executive assistant who worked at a previous organization restricted access to the CEO, and she remained relatively isolated from other voices or perspectives. New to the non-profit sector, she believed she was operating with successful business practices that would transfer into any work setting.

In reality, her new organizational culture had a history of participatory and collegial management. Dictating changes to the organization not only made her unpopular, it eventually made her unable to accomplish her goals. Work production and confidence levels fell to all-time lows. Many long-term employees took early retirements and the new hires she made left within a year. There was a revolving door at some of the most critical positions within the organization.

The communication problems persisted as press reports and communications to the Board of Directors were carefully managed, and dissent from those who worked within the organization was not permitted to be heard at the highest levels. A climate of fear emerged due to the strength of her political allies.

This is an example of the wrong leadership style for the environment. The new CEO came into a leadership role without thinking about fit. She was leading with the wrong leadership style for the work environment. Her board hired a coach from the field to help her through the difficulties and sent her to two leadership development boot camps. In analyzing what went wrong, her strongest role model had been her father who was a micro-manager in his business. When this woman's ultimate leadership moment arrived, she took on the characteristics she had learned as a young woman and modeled her behavior on that of her father. Her father's business had been relatively small; the family and a few close managers had been his inner circle. Using her father's approach in a large organization meant the CEO interacted with only a few people in the inner circle. She was not leading from inclusiveness and rarely seen in any "walk around" management situations where others could communicate with her informally. Her personality style was more introverted and aloof.

Contrast this style to someone who is more experienced in a teamwork environment and confident enough in her abilities to acknowledge she cannot perform every task. The confident leader knows she must respect and rely on the expertise of others to accomplish the organization's mutual goals as she clearly communicates the vision. The CEO in the previous leadership example had not developed a style beyond her personal history and personality type. She was on a collision course within the organization from the beginning. Her inexperience in a nonprofit environment and lack of previous leadership development was a formula for failure. Most successful organizations are stronger than any one ineffective leader, but I wonder how much further forward this nonprofit could have moved with a more sophisticated leader that was a fit for the environment.

———————

STRONG WOMAN PRESIDENT MEETS A CRISIS SUCCESSFULLY USING COMMUNICATION SKILLS AND A TEAM ORIENTATION

Several years ago, I met the president of a historic higher education institution in Virginia. She spoke at a Statewide Leadership Conference for women, and it was clear she was a role model for many in the room. During her comments, she described a recent fire that had consumed one of the institution's historic residence halls that also served as an office for faculty. The president received a call late one night that a fire had begun on campus, and she rushed to the campus.

During her speech to the women, she spoke in detail about her responses to the fire that night. News reports had said the president was at scene, but we heard that as soon as she arrived, she called in her leadership team and set up a communications hub. They tracked down missing students to make sure everyone was safe; immediately set up a web page to keep parents and others updated on a frequent basis; called faculty members whose offices were consumed by the fire; and kept in touch with her board, firefighters, police, press, anxious parents, students, and many others throughout the night and into the successive days.

They did everything possible to keep a broad public informed about what was happening, as it was happening, and she was highly visible throughout this crisis, making sure everyone was safe and then reassuring the community that the devastation would be addressed as quickly as possible.

As one of her peers told me after the president's presentation, "she is one of the best communicators I have ever seen in action." The president met the crisis and her team helped her solve the issues. However, this president's communication skills did not start with the fire crisis, but had become her trademark in day-to-day and weekly interactions with her leadership teams. When she first began her presidency, this woman spent a significant amount of time to develop a team mentality. She began with the premise that she wanted them all to become stronger professionals while working on her team. She understood that if the team succeeded, she would also be successful in her role. For example, every year during her vacation time, the president took time to think about each of her staff members and begin to find ways to grow the staff with additional training. She built the competence of her leadership team and took intentional steps to improve their communication with one another in the team meetings. If there were a disagreement between two team members, they solved it immediately after the meeting, and she ensured they had time to work together to learn to understand and respect the other's viewpoint. She was able to move her institution forward by using strong communication and everyone in the state was talking about her effective leadership style.

As a final thought to the two examples above, obviously there are times when a decision must be made quickly because of a crisis or a timing issue. These are the moments when the leader in a democratic or participatory environment must take on the "command and control" style of leadership. Good leadership is about both being "in tune" with the environment, and flexible enough to adapt to the environment and conditions when a crisis management point arises. However, since organizational cultures are very slow to change after a "command and control crisis moment," all leaders must adapt to the communication and leadership style that has proven most successful within the existing culture. It is about fit.

On the way to your own leadership positions, it is also important for you to build managerial competence. The *Sixth Principle of Leadership* relates to acquiring these managerial experiences as well. I always suggest that women seek opportunities to manage people, projects, and budgets and to build a track record of accomplishments and skills.

No one strict set of leadership style or managerial rules are absolute. To believe so is part of inexperience in leadership and work situations. Flexibility, depending on circumstance and conditions, is a key to success. It has just been in the past 25 years that more leadership positions have opened up for women. Many have worked a long time to reach the opportunity to move into upper management and leadership roles.

As we discussed, when women finally arrive in the leadership role they sometimes try to model behaviors that are not consistent with their own personality types. The saying, "To thine own self be true," is important to remember here. Early in your life find leaders and leadership characteristics that you want to emulate, then when the leadership moment arrives, you will be ready and not make unintentional mistakes. Long term, each of us should take some time to analyze leadership opportunities when they become available to us. Remember that to be successful, you should look for options that allow you to use your own skills and strengths.

CHAPTER SEVEN

Find a Mentor/ Be a Mentor

*The Seventh Career Principle Is to Form a
Relationship With a Trusted Counselor*

In our action-oriented world, the word mentor is no longer just a noun but has transformed into a verb. It refers to a pattern of behavior or a process where one person serves as a mentor or a guide to another, and it is the seventh principle.

Mentoring is widely discussed in corporations, schools, and youth programs as a method of developing talented individuals for future leadership opportunities in our communities. It is definitely not a new concept. Many sources believe the word mentor comes from the ancient Greeks, as "Mentor" was the teacher in the story of Ulysses, the king in ancient history, and subject of Homer's *Odyssey*.[1] When Ulysses left on his epic journey during the ten-year Trojan War, he left his son to the care of "Mentor," his trusted friend.

It is an old concept with a very contemporary application in our high tech and high touch world. As our work and social lives have changed and now include significant relationships developed through technological/electronic means, it is important to have a mentor, a trusted counselor or guide. A mentor can help you consider actions and communications that will keep you on track or serve as a braking mechanism before you make a mistake. For example, talking and thinking things over with a mentor enables you to briefly slow up on a possibly "too speedy" decision you might regret in the long term. In most cases, having a mentor is co-related to success.

Women have not always been recognized for being mentors to one another. In fact as recently as 20 years ago, many women who were in a position of power blocked other women from becoming successful in the workplace. It turned out that the women who originally broke through the glass ceiling often had a man for a mentor.

THREE OLDER WOMEN BLOCK AN EMERGING LEADER

Today, Bev is one of the most successful leaders in the work environment and is widely recognized for her vision and teamwork. However, when I first met Bev, a woman 20 years her senior was holding her back and took credit for all of the young woman's recent work. The older woman and two others in the same unit had emerged as a power nexus in an area of the business that was historically marginalized and their behaviors went mostly unnoticed.

Bev had proposed a new process that would affect all clients throughout the business and would definitely lead to increased recognition for the organization as a leader in their industry segment. Senior management decided the new business process was an exceptional idea. The corporate headquarters decided to hire a new, senior male executive to implement the program and to solve the unit's declining customer numbers.

What he found after several months was that three older women had entrenched themselves by holding all of the internal leadership positions. Their goal was to hang on until retirement by blocking all other women who entered the environment. None of these women had ever married or developed lives beyond their workplace. They socialized together and were widely known across the business units as isolated. Our young professional woman received the worst work schedules and was blocked from any attempts to improve her status through continuing education. Once the new executive was in place, there was much angst as the three women tried to intimidate the outside executive. However after three years, he had moved the three women out of their pivotal assignments and eventually all three retired.

After their departure, Bev received the opportunity to work part-time and finish her education. The male senior executive served eight years as leader and then stepped aside into pre-retirement roles within the business. Fast forward 20 years later, and Bev has moved into the primary leadership role and grown an organizational segment that is the largest within the corporation. It is widely respected by other businesses and recognized as a team environment. All new employees hired by Bev are now assigned a mentor to ensure a smooth transition so they will ultimately have every opportunity to become successful themselves.

Why did it take a man to come into the organization to straighten out this unit? Were the older women insecure and afraid that they would lose power in the workplace if they assisted another woman to implement new innovative plans? Had their work lives become too important to their self-images and too personal? Fortunately, now that women are in most workspaces, this pattern of behavior is not as prevalent. As women, we must assist others for us all to find more equality at work. If you are confident in your own abilities, why fear other women who can join your efforts and make everyone more successful in the mission of the organization? Most men seem to know it is important to mentor for succession planning and for the best talent to rise and move the business forward.

Contemporary businesses recognize that mentoring is an excellent way to nurture and retain talent. Organizations have established formalized mentoring programs as part of their human resources planning. This type of program makes sense when you consider the costs per hire that organizations devote to recruitment of new employees. From a business perspective, it is better to retain and develop talent than to always be recruiting new talent.

Mentoring helps organizations develop new leaders with the right skills for the organization. It can put high potential individuals on a fast track. Mentoring can also help promote diversity by helping new employees adjust into the organization. In a recent study of mid- and upper level executives, research found that executives credited mentors as contributing to their success. In fact, 44% of women credited someone at work as their mentor, and 50% of both men and women said their mentor was their life partner.

In other research related to retaining people in the science fields, a study found that having a mentor in college or early in one's career has a crucial impact on staying in the field. It also showed that men and women receive mentoring at significantly different rates with more men than women utilizing both formal and informal networking.[2]

It is the informal relationships that develop more naturally between two people, without organizational input and strict process guidelines, that I want to focus on as they are accessible to everyone. In these cases, a mentor can be a relative, friend, former colleague, teacher, or supervisor. Finding a mentor will usually help you to see the "big picture" of your career and current job and to avoid possible problem areas. A mentor is usually an older, more experienced individual who helps and guides another's development. Anyone could potentially be a mentor and every successful person should consider the concept of helping the next person in line.

YOUNG WOMAN FINDS A MENTOR AND IS LED TO A NEW CAREER PATH

As a young mother of three, Maria was looking for employment that would provide her family with benefits. She had a degree in business and originally came to the United States from Puerto Rico. She had strong technology skills, a multicultural perspective, and untapped talent when first hired at the university by a woman leader who just returned to academia from working in the corporate arena. It quickly became clear this young woman was flexible, as she took on multiple roles as needed in the unit, and was an enthusiastic worker with enough emotional intelligence to survive. The director knew that it would take a strong customer business orientation and energy to grow a neglected part of the institution. Maria had all the characteristics of someone who could become a strong player for her unit, and she enjoyed working with students in higher education.

However, it was not until four years later that this young professional began to consider building a career in higher education. She put off pursuing her master's degree several times when it was suggested, during performance evaluations, until her boss made it a requirement to move forward in the unit. Without the master's Maria was going to have a very difficult time leaving the administrative assistant role and moving into a permanent professional position. After gaining admission to graduate school, Maria entered a mentoring role with her director. She needed the self-confidence that she could succeed in college during her middle years and balance her work, family, and new role as a non-traditional adult student. Her director had been in the same position some years earlier and it made sense for Maria to find a professional who could guide her through the process.

Maria had become committed to the education field and had great faculty to guide her professional studies, but it was the mentoring that gave Maria the initial confidence and on-going support through the four multi-tasking years. During those years, Maria's children grew up and entered college themselves. Her children also occasionally interacted with Maria's mentor. Imagine the sense of accomplishment that everyone felt at the time of Maria's graduation. Maria found a career that provided satisfaction and the mentor felt she had passed on knowledge to a new generation of emerging women leaders. It will be interesting to see what she can accomplish.

At different times of your life, different mentors are appropriate. To get started, be observant. Who are the role models in your field or your life? Are there particular professionals you admire and respect? Whomever you identify, you will actually need to approach this individual and say something such as, "I would like to learn from your experience and spend some time speaking to you and learning from you." It is important for both parties to establish and develop a sense of rapport that can lead to open and honest communication.

While this type of mentoring is not part of a formalized program, both participants need to realize they are entering into a special relationship. If you hesitate to ask someone to help you, remember what Winston Churchill said, "We make a living by what we get, but we make a life by what we give." Many people would like to assist you as a mentor but you need to ask them.

_____

MENTORING RELATIONSHIPS ARE RECIPROCAL

I know that seeking out someone to become a mentor may seem awkward at first. I actually put this advice into practice in my own life, and overcame my introverted nature by talking to a vice president of Student Affairs, at the insistence of a mutual friend. I asked if he would consider becoming my mentor during my return to school for a doctorate. It was difficult to ask for personalized help, but it was also important for me to have a mentor as I restarted my career. This mentor became a role model for me. He had years of experience in my field, and was one of my teachers while I was working on my degree. He was most generous with his time and made it possible for us to spend at least one hour a week talking about the field while I was interning in his office. While there were established goals for the conversations, he also made it an open-ended conversation to insure that I was able to ask ad hoc questions about the day-to-day events in our field at the local level. It was quite a learning experience.

Several years after my graduation and that time of intense mentoring, my mentor left the university to teach at two other institutions. Our mentoring relationship continued, though more sporadically, for four more years through telephone and occasional dinner meetings. The relationship was reciprocal as eventually we helped each other by discussing issues in the field at our respective places of employment. I asked him for advice and he was a reference for me as I began my work; at one point in this mentoring relationship, I was able to serve as a reference for him. Mentoring can be a way of giving back to your profession. My mentor had a mentor of his own and his work with students was a way of "returning the favor" or passing it on to the next generation in his field.

After the first few years in my career, the relationship began to decline and now we have minimal contact. Other mentors have taken his place as my career has moved forward. However, a mentor can always stay on as an advisor, in the background, throughout your lifetime for networking and periodic "career" checkups.

Mentoring can take place in person, over the telephone, or through e-mail; communication is not bound by geographical considerations or even time. It can be completed as one-on-one mentoring or in a small group. Many organizations and communities have groups of young professionals or new residents that meet for the purposes of mutual support. When a more experienced employee or someone from the established culture enters into the equation, the group may move from mutual support by your peers to a mentor and a mentoring group. With the help of a guide, the new culture can be explained, questioned, and understood more quickly.

If you are interested in forming either a mentoring relationship or a mentoring group, you may wonder about the characteristics of good mentoring. The previous examples hinted at several. For best practices, the relationships should:
- Be mutual and reciprocal
- Not necessarily have a distinct beginning and/or ending
- Evolve into lifelong networking
- Usually be limited in time commitment but move forward with periodic contact.

In a successful mentoring relationship, each of us takes responsibility for our own life and decisions, but we expand our thinking by discussing work and personal related issues with others. Mentoring gives us another perspective. You will ask for advice and guidance from a mentor, but not for answers. Remember that a mentor does not want to hear just the negatives and be your stress relief. They also want to celebrate your accomplishments and help you consider career development issues.

For those who develop mentoring relationships, your trusted advisor can provide both a safety net and support, and decrease the stress of a new job, situation, or challenge. Talking with a mentor is definitely the place to test out your new ideas and receive feedback in a private forum. Your mentor can help you with selecting career options and can definitely accelerate your learning and productivity on a job. Advice may include discussions about continuing education and/or skill development. A typical question to your mentor might be, "If you were where I am now, what would you be thinking about doing?"

There are some limitations for mentoring relationships. For instance, confidential and ethical items may be out of bounds. Either the mentor or the mentee can say, "While I want to continue to assist you or work with you, this is not an area I am comfortable exploring." Honesty is a key!

For the individual who becomes the "mentor" in the relationship, it is about the personal satisfaction of assisting others. The relationship creates an opportunity to leave a legacy by sharing their experience and wisdom. How many times in life do we get to pass positive energy forward? As the comedian, Dick Gregory said, "One of the things I keep learning is that the secret to being happy is doing things for other people."[3] However, while discussing issues with a younger colleague it also forces the mentor into self-reflection and can reaffirm their own approach to issues. It can expand their personal perspective and insights.

Mentoring relationships have a lifespan, and it is important to know when to move on. Remember that just as you have many roles throughout your life, which are prioritized differently at life stages, you will also need various mentors at different times. When you are just beginning your education or professional life, the mentor may be a teacher, an experienced colleague, or your first supervisor. As you evolve and grow, the mentoring need may change. In our actively evolving world, the lifespan of an active mentorship could be just one to two years as things change quickly. The beginning and end of an informal mentoring relationship may not be distinct, but it is important to thank people for their assistance. Using common courtesy and expressing appreciation for their help can go a long way as you continue to evolve and network in a global marketplace. Finally, if you consider becoming a mentor, "The more you lose yourself in something bigger than yourself, the more energy you will have." Norman Vincent Peale[4].

CHAPTER EIGHT

Be Proactive in Job Search Strategy

*The Eight Career Principle Is to Develop and Update Strategy to
Be Ready for New Opportunities*

The best and brightest professionals manage their own upward mobility with a focus on networking, strong resumes, and learning how to utilize recruiters effectively. It is important to know *how* to find a job.

There is a strategy, which has changed dramatically as technology has made it possible to network with others more easily, find employment opportunities around the world, and complete critical job research quickly and efficiently. Given the speed of contemporary job searches, my advice to women is to always have your resume and other credentials ready for the unexpected opportunity, and be prepared to take advantage of all networking.

Think about it—when was the last time you updated your resume or found a new job? If you answered more than two years ago, you are out of date. Associate an annual resume check-up with some important event in your life *every year*. Many of us plan for an annual visit to the doctor for a physical or we think about our accomplishments once a year during a performance review. It's also just as important for you to add to and/or modify your resume at least once a year. This technique can ensure good career management.

If you are ready to begin an active career management strategy, my top five resume development tips include the following:
- Before beginning to write, spend time thinking about your accomplishments during the last one to ten years and use the *problem, action, result* rubric for organizing your thoughts.
- Capture key words that market and brand you and place in a line at the top of the resume immediately after your contact information.

- Make your "sell" to your reader in a brief section that focuses on previous experience, core competencies, skills, and other unique characteristics that define you and your career goals.
- Quantify your accomplishments and link them to the next position you seek.
- Be a minimalist as you write, be positive, and do not use the same words as every other candidate.

People who are meticulous about keeping their business plans in order often ignore the habit of keeping our personal documents current. We may spend hours each year planning goals and objectives for an organization and yet never seem to get around to doing the same for ourselves. Remember, a current resume to send out quickly, without major rewriting or restructuring, should be part of every woman's portfolio. It helps quicken the response time to new opportunities. This quote helps me keep up with this commitment, "The important thing is this: …To be able at any moment to sacrifice what we are for what we could become." (Quote by Charles Dubois)[1] To me, it means you never know when the next great job opportunity may occur.

Your resume is just one small piece of the job search process, and part of a larger career management strategy that women need to understand and use. For all of us, networking is the most powerful job search technique we can use. In my consulting practice, if I ask a room full of people, "How did you find your last job?" many in the audience will respond that someone told them about their current position. The stories in the room vary—a family member or best friend pointed them to an organization, or a previous colleague referred them to a new position.

MEET TWO EXPERT USERS OF SOCIAL MEDIA AND
NETWORKING FOR CAREER MANAGEMENT PURPOSES

Chris was a student of mine in the early 1990s and has since developed an outstanding career in human resources management, focused on organizational and leadership development, while working at three major Fortune 100 companies. With exceptional interpersonal skills, she learned over the years to build a strong professional network of colleagues by staying in touch with them periodically, and is always ready to assist when needed. She managed this in the early years through occasional telephone calls or dinner/lunch meetings; in the past few years, it has evolved into a strong presence in social media and specifically LinkedIn.

Chris makes frequent posts to LinkedIn about leadership development books or conferences to keep her presence in front of the network of professionals that has come together at this site. It's not hard to think of this individual when new opportunities arise. The quality and depth of her work in the field is there for all to see and utilize in similar work situations. Chris shares ideas freely with her network.

I have been impressed at the concise entries she makes on a consistent basis. She has also been able to establish enough frequency to keep you interested but not so much that you want to delete anything that comes in posted from this individual. She has carved out "the balance" of using this new media for professional development but not strayed over a line of overuse that makes you want to delete everything on the computer screen. Finding the balance and the appropriate usage of social media sites is a new critically important area of career management and job search strategy.

Another friend, Laura, is the best networker I have encountered in the last ten years; she has crossed geographic boundaries by building a strong network that began with her college affiliation and year of graduation. While Laura lives in a rural environment, she has used Facebook to reconnect with old friends from her alma mater around the world. She has told me stories about colleagues in China, Paris, and the Middle East for the last five years. Laura utilizes this friendship group to accomplish some of the most amazing projects in her region.

As a pioneer of Facebook usage, Laura has set the bar for all of us. I don't think in the beginning she really understood the power her affiliation group could have for her career and the causes she chose to support. Again, like Chris, Laura has used her conversational capabilities, her genuineness, and persuasive powers, and translated these to her online presence and moved her career forward several times.

Last year she impressed her bosses when she created an event and raised significant funds for a non-profit almost exclusively by using Facebook. People showed up from all over the country for the event and the costs of staging the event were much lower than normal. She understood the population she needed to reach was computer savvy by age and profession, then used technology to stage an unbelievable event that reached more participants with less overhead. The participants in her Facebook group even voted on several new fundraising ideas before the planning got started, so Laura knew the event she developed would have traction and ensure success. She eliminated formal invitations and postage, thus there was no need for an administrative assistant to tally the event participants, as this was automatic with the software.

Laura has also set limits for herself about how she uses her network and her online community. For example, she does not post without thinking through her goals and confidentiality issues. She is intentional with every entry. She always uses a word document to correct text, then cuts and paste into the site for accuracy and quality control.

The power of technology for career management and networking purposes is "scary" because you can reach so many people with both positive and negative impressions, but these women have become "stars" and managed the technology to their advantage, both personally and professionally.

Besides using technology to enhance your career management plans, here are some other career and job search tips from my years of working with people who make successful career transitions:

- Technology should be a beginning point of everyone's active job search to locate openings and perform initial research.
- Utilize both online and in-person networking strategies as your top job search technique.
- In addition to your resume, update your reference lists with people who can share a variety of perspectives on your work and include current contact information.
- Everyone should develop and add to a professional portfolio that includes project samples, letters from customers, performance evaluations, awards and training documentation, and use this to present your case for a promotion or at evaluation times.
- Develop contacts with recruiting and employment agencies in your field of interest.
- Develop a target list of 5 to 10 organizations that are a good match for your experience and future goals every year after re-writing your resume.
- When actively seeking a new opportunity, make applications to advertised listings and tap into the hidden and unadvertised employment opportunities found through personal research and your networking.

Developing a job search strategy that includes most of the suggestions above will help you make a career transition to another organization or achieve a promotion within your organization more efficiently. However, did you know that most people when they need to make a job change revert to spending hours of their time reading the job advertisements available to larger audiences? They take a passive approach to career management rather than an active approach.

Responding to posted advertisements is the least effective method of finding employment and contrasts dramatically with the techniques of networking, targeting, the use of electronic databases, or recruitment firms, which are more effective. You should learn to use all of the strategies effectively.

Did you know that as your career progresses the statistics related to the effectiveness of networking as an employment strategy increase dramatically? In entry-level jobs, networking may account for only about 30% of all jobs found, however, by the time you move to mid-level management or senior positions this percentage increases to 60%. Networking is the single most powerful job search technique for both employers and employees. A recent survey of national companies, asked about their current recruiting strategies, found that the most frequently utilized strategies are related to networking online or in-person, employee referrals, followed closely by social media and the internet.

I have explained the networking technique many times in executive coaching sessions and found that the notion of talking to other people to locate your next opportunity, or to understand where unadvertised openings may be, always receives mixed reviews. For those people who are brought up to be independent and self-reliant, the idea that they may be asking for "help" is unthinkable. I try to make sure these people focus on networking as an information gathering process rather than viewing it asking for a favor or help. Also, for those people that find interacting in social situations more difficult, networking will not be their first choice when beginning a job search. They tend to seek the more passive methods like online job applications.

SOFTWARE ENGINEER USES TECHNOLOGY TO NETWORK

One of my former clients, a computer programmer who was very introverted, found several unique ways to use technology to help her network and track the results of her conversations in the job search process. This person was terrified about networking, although she knew it was one of the most critical strategies to use in any job search. She knew that even in technology related fields, it is important to be able to communicate verbally with customers and colleagues, so we decided to work together to find a comfort zone for her networking strategy and one that she could use later in her work situation.

Our compromise strategy got her to do most of her networking on the telephone rather than in a person and included a script for talking to people during the job search that she displayed on her computer screen during telephone conversations. This adaptation made the networking more comfortable and part of the client's normal routine of working with technology, because she knew what basic ideas she needed to cover in any networking situation.

She identified initial employment options by researching online in employment databases and at organizational websites. Then she networked with others she knew in the field to get a perspective on the identified organization's work culture and to find someone who worked within the organization who she could call directly about the advertised openings. She always followed the directions for applying online, but her conversations with those who had a perspective on the organization helped her identify "best fit" options for herself and also helped her know how to highlight her experiences on the application.

Since this search was extensive, she tracked every conversation she had during her networking and research process on an Excel spreadsheet she developed. Any time she got a call back from an application or networking conversation, she could immediately expand her tracking system and see where she was in that specific application process with dates applied, the names of people with whom she had spoken, other names of secondary contacts they had given her, and much more. Her skills in technology were emphasized in this search and she was able to find a way to play to her strengths.

What most of us find in a networking situation is that people actually like to talk about their work and are often very generous with their time and contact list when given an opportunity. Networking is really nothing more than talking to people and asking them for their opinion about your next employment option. You are asking for advice. Networking can be done within your family, social, and professional circles. It should be handled with respect for the other person's time constraints, in a confidential manner, and in a setting that you are both comfortable.

I have seen effective networking take place in classrooms, boardrooms, offices, golf courses, coffee shops, Chamber of Commerce events, lockers rooms, and so on. The important first element is to be comfortable with the process. Where do you meet others with whom you like to talk? For my mother's generation it was over coffee and tea or at the bridge table while for my daughters it is via e-mail or at a weekend barbeque. The process across the generations, however, remains relatively stable.

You ask the other person to give you some advice and explain your situation quickly and positively. If you have booked an appointment for this business, be sure to bring a copy of your resume or bio. Do not dwell on the past but ask for advice about the future. It is important for you to show sincerity, listen carefully, ask open-ended questions, follow-up, and thank people for their time and consideration.

I usually tell my clients to work at networking with the "2 by 4" principle. If you can have two conversations, they can lead you to four additional contacts. To incorporate this method, at the end of every conversation ask if there are other people to whom you should be speaking at this point. We have all heard about the relative small world we live in and that all of us are only several layers of conversations away from being able to make contact with someone famous like Kevin Bacon or the current U.S. president.

In a good networking job search strategy, it is important to have enough of these conversations; I suggest from 20 to 30 to get a job search started. Why? Because there is about a 25% return rate in any job search, and you need to create enough volume to get offers. You need to generate enough leads and make enough applications so at the end of the job search, you will have enough options available for your decision-making and next career steps.

Your networking conversations with others can lead you to develop a list of targeted organizations to pursue in the job search. There is also a distinct strategy to use in the targeting phase of a job search. You will want to learn as much as you can about each organization you target; I recommend that you use a 360° approach. You will want to learn about an organization from many perspectives. Go online and review an organization's website, talk to people who used to or currently work at the organization. Speak to customers of the organization or suppliers to the organization. Your goal is to gain as much information as possible to help you decide if this organization might indeed be a good place for you to work and a target of your search.

In the process of networking and targeting organizations, you will begin the unconscious matching process of deciding whether a company/organization is a good fit. Finding the "fit" is another key element to a great job search. I always coach people to look for opportunities that are a good match for them. First and foremost, you will need to feel some empathy or have a strong interest in the goals of the organization. We know that people are successful who enjoy their work and share a passion for the organizational mission. It really is true that people who love what they do are usually successful at work.

Your fit also must include an analysis of how you blend with the corporate culture. Many hiring and promotion decisions are ultimately influenced by the notion of fit. In deciding hiring and promotions, a manager will weigh the elements of previous experience, skill sets, and desire or motivation, but the idea of "fit" is the one that can ultimately lead to an offer. Do you fit with the organizational goals? Are you a good fit with other employees in the organization? Is your working style a fit for the supervisor's style? If you have done a good job of analyzing your fit into an organization, you can reach your objective.

One suggestion I make is to analyze the job description or advertisement and honestly look at your resume to see if you meet the qualifications posted. If you meet all but one or two, I suggest you stretch and apply. However, if you only meet one of the six posted criteria or qualifications, I think you should continue to search for a better match. Many job searches are derailed by rejection and the lowered self-esteem that comes from applying for employment opportunities that are not a good fit.

During networking and targeting conversations, the name of a recruiter or employment agency may come up often. Please do take note. Recruiting organizations can account for one third of job matches and definitely should be part of everyone's job search and career management strategy. It is particularly true as your career progresses, as you gain specializations, and as your salary increases. Third party agencies and recruiters are specialized and available for many fields including engineering, education, accounting, healthcare, and more. While it makes sense to integrate these into your job search, always remain in control of the relationships. Remember recruiters are paid to find a talented professional and their loyalty is to the person or organization that is covering the bottom line. No matter how personable a recruiting individual is, how many times they have assisted you and your colleagues, or how sincere they are in wanting to assist in your search, you must always remember to remain in control of the final employment decisions. Once the employment contracts are signed and the recruiter is gone, you will be the one employed that first day. If this organization or job is not a good fit for you, it will be your problem and not that of the employment agency or recruiter.

TWO RECRUITING STORIES FROM THE ENGINEERING AND EDUCATION PROFESSIONS WITH STRONG MESSAGES

One of my clients, a female engineer, moved from her former employer, General Electric, to a competitor and ended up having to repay the organization for the recruiter's fee. She was recruited for the position and was very excited because the company's headquarters was closer to her family and she was going to be making more money. After successfully interviewing and receiving an offer, the engineer signed a document that said if she had to leave within the first year of her employment, she would be required to repay the employer the money they had spent on the recruiter's fee. She signed thinking she would never leave since she had received everything she wanted in her negotiations. However life has a way of changing everything in a moment, and when this woman's husband was diagnosed with a serious illness she wanted to leave her job for at least a year.

This personal dilemma for my client was in no way the recruiter's fault. However, it does point out that when you enter into employment negotiations with an employer, remember to read all of the "fine print" in your contract agreements. This employer used a recruiter and the fee was charged against the new employee for one year, which meant in reality that both the employee and the employer paid for the recruiter's fee the first year. Always follow the dollar.

———————

A second client of mine worked with a recruiting firm that specialized in higher education placements. She was ready for a step up from a director's position at a small regional institution to a director's position at a much larger institution with a national reputation. The recruitment process included an initial screening and interview by the recruitment agency, then a telephone interview with the on-campus search committee, and finally a two-day interview process with all of the on-campus stakeholders.

The process was smooth and transparent to my client until the on-campus interview visit. Although my client and the recruiter discussed the job description and institutional needs for the new director in detail, it became apparent the recruiter had not mentioned, and may not have known, additional criteria that were not listed in the official job search materials. During the interview, my client was asked if she had any difficulty working with diversity. The institution had a diverse population by race, age, and ethnicity. The staff was very diverse and the final question on the second day of interviews, behind closed doors with the supervisor, was, "Can you work with people of a different race?"

Although this woman gave a strong answer related to diversity to the full interview committee and to the private question asked at the end of the process, it was clear the position's hiring decision was going to be based on fit. Several days later, the recruiter called to deliver the institution's hiring decision and her words were, "it was about fit."

The strong message here is that even a recruiter may not have all of the facts; it is incumbent on all job seekers to research the organizational needs at a variety of levels.

CHAPTER NINE

Use the Fine Art of Self-Promotion

*The Ninth Career Principle Is to Know How to Advance Your Career
When Relocation Is Impossible*

How many of us are part of a dual career couple? How many are so entrenched in one community by our personal lives that we cannot leave to find a promotion or new job? Probably 75% of us have to factor in our non-work lives when we make career decisions. There are many questions every woman has to answer when she determines whether to move her career forward in the same location or relocate to find another position. She has to decide when her career needs should lead her choices or when her family needs must lead. Is this her time to leave or stay? She must think about finding time to stay healthy—physically, mentally, and spiritually. Will she have more time, if she moves? When women strive to find balance between work-life, family-life and self-needs, it becomes complicated.

I am frequently asked, "How can I build my career within my current organization since I cannot leave this location to find a new position?" I encourage people to understand and value the choices they made and to move forward with vigor to find career and life satisfaction in their current location. One of my answers to building a career in one place is to learn to implement the "art" of self-promotion by managing yourself as an entrepreneur when interacting with your employer. It is a critical skill that can help you achieve career satisfaction while you balance your multiple life roles.

While humility is good in small doses and concern for our life roles is essential, I believe women must learn to market themselves in their career world. I've found that many women are unable to advocate effectively on their own behalf in their work. Part of the reason for their inaction is a result of societal messages about gender appropriate behaviors. Women receive messages about how to implement gender in society that we see in the media or as we travel. Cultures vary in their expectations and treatment of women. We know that many societies still require women to interact with their childbearing functions through very restrictive patterns of behavior. Many cultures do not reward assertive independent women. Women are unsure when, or if, it is appropriate to put their work-life on an equal balance with family responsibilities and they put their personal needs last.

We have a history of women in the workplace that includes unequal access to types of job functions based on gender and to salaries that pay a fraction of what men receive for equal standards of labor. It was just in the last fifty years that the workplace statistics changed dramatically, and they now show most women are working in full-time jobs outside of the home in the United States. We now consider women working and their employment as the new normal. Work is major life role. Employment can bring a sense of purpose and satisfaction to women as it is not just about adding to the family income. Because this migration of women to the workplace is a recent development, it is small wonder that some women still cannot lobby effectively on their own behalf. I have been amazed at how this continues even with some of the most accomplished of us.

Interestingly, the need for self-promotion and management is not a usual part of conversations I have with men. When we talk about how to approach a boss for a new position and a raise, most men know they must actively market themselves to rise through an organization and move on to the next steps in their career ladder. While family and life considerations can be part of the equation with men, they self-promote without self-imposed limitations or the need to answer internal questions about self.

MEET MARY ANN FROM NEW JERSEY

Just at the beginning of the telecommunications boom,

Mary Ann contacted me for some help. She worked for her employer for 10 years and needed assistance, as she was unable to get a promotion within her organization. In reviewing her career, I learned she had originally been hired as an administrative assistant at a major employer in her geographic region. Both Mary Ann and her husband worked at the same company. During her employment, she had earned a Bachelor's and Master's degree after hours. She knew she was capable of more responsibilities at work.

However, each time she applied for another internal position at a new level and pay scale, she wasn't called for an interview. In reviewing her resume and discussing her professional accomplishments, it was obvious she needed to articulate what she learned in her academic programs and how her new skills could be utilized in another position.

Mary Ann assumed, because she had received excellent performance evaluations from her immediate supervisor, everyone within the corporation knew she was capable of success in a new expanded, managerial job function. I shared with Mary Ann that one of the most difficult career moves is to transform ourselves from one function to another distinct function within the same organization.

This requires the employer to see you in a new frame of reference. To accomplish this, you must market yourself and make sure your job search tools, including the resume, two-minute personal introduction, and responses to interview questions, all explain your accomplishments. These tools will demonstrate you have the experience and skills to move to the next level. You must highlight skills that will follow you into the new position. If you are trying to do something new and different, like Mary Ann, you will need to talk in terms of "like" and "as."

Here is an example of how Mary Ann and I changed her marketing strategy. Her marketing tools included comments such as—"What I did before is *like or similar to what you need* (explain and give examples)." "In the new position, *just as I was successful* utilizing my skills of…I can utilize these in this new opportunity." "If you combine my previous skills with what I have learned in my job here and my new skills which are…, I am confident I can be successful in this new position."

We worked through two additional internal job searches, but Mary Ann was still not a serious contender for an internal promotion. The company could not see her beyond the administrative assistant role. Ultimately, after much conversation about what was important to her at this moment in time, Mary Ann took an entry-level management position with a competitor within driving distance of her home. She was fortunate as the telecommunications industry was expanding and she was in an urban area with multiple employment targets nearby. Mary Ann found a new environment where people could understand what she was capable of achieving. Her long-term goal was to work with the competitor and use these new experiences to leverage herself back to the former employer in a few years. Sometimes you must leave to move forward.

This client's flexibility to move upward by changing employers is not always possible for many women who are anchored to a specific location because of their other roles and responsibilities.

The following self-promotion strategies can be incorporated into your current work role to help you move forward:

Step One: Develop Your Brand and Implement a Marketing Plan

Think about this quote by Christopher M. Knight, "You must have mindshare before you can have market share."[1] This means people have to *think about you* before they will "buy" or promote you and "your brand" at work. The phrase, "The Brand Called You," was coined in the 1990's by Tom Peters,[2] a well-known business author and consultant. He also understood that in contemporary workplaces we would be marketing our own unique brands to others. Remember, that no matter what your long-term career plan, you must communicate positively about your own work in order to achieve your goals. So how do others know about your performance at work? The answer is communication.

Most of us do not think our work actually involves marketing, but we all must be marketers of our unique brand that includes our previous experience, accomplishments, skills, and personal qualities. Don't assume, like Mary Ann, that your organization knows the good work you are doing. This becomes more difficult the longer you are involved in any particular organization or job function. We believe that our work, "speaks for itself" or that "people here know what I do."

To create your marketing plan, first identify who the customers are for this information about you. Who needs to be listening? How could you communicate, through a variety of media, what you do and how well you do it? Should your self-marketing be made in-person or through social media? Prepare a list of different groups that need to know what you do and what achievements you've made. Have you been communicating effectively with these groups?

Whenever you are involved in marketing yourself, it is important to stay attuned to people's attention span so they receive your message. Remember in self-promotion you need to:

- Build rapport and find common ground.
- Keep your marketing message short and to the point.
- Remember repetition is the key to learning and three times should complete the task. You don't want to sound like a worn-out recording in the room.
- Speak in terms that they can understand—use the same language.
- Know what motivates your listener.

Step Two: Take on Additional Responsibilities at Your Job

I suggest that women seek out and take on additional responsibilities within the current employer's structure when they want to demonstrate new skills. However, you will need to be selective with this strategy. You always want to be successful on any new project and not over commit so that your current job suffers.

For example, one woman, who found a promotion in a higher education environment of 27,000 students and 2,000 employees, decided she must meet more key faculty and administrators beyond her reporting lines. It was such a big school she had become lost. She worked daily to deliver one of the campus student services, but was involved with only a small percentage of the overall population. She was so busy working, she failed to meet colleagues in other departments and colleges.

To become better known, she chose to apply for a university committee seeking volunteers and worked on a campus-wide team to develop future goals and objectives for the university. By taking on this assignment, she was seen as someone with global and future-oriented ideas, and in the eyes of the community, she moved beyond the limited scope of her daily responsibilities. She took on many extra hours in committee meetings and developed new networking contacts that could help not only in her current responsibilities, but especially when she decided to seek an internal promotion. It was a lot of extra work, but several years later, she did get a promotion and a higher salary.

Remember at work, as in the rest of life, it comes down to relationships that you can call on for information and assistance. This is especially true when you are seeking advancement, as you will get multiple perspectives on possible new roles and have a variety of people who can serve as a reference. Become more visible, develop relationships with decision makers, and meet the people who can hire you into the next level. Rarely will relationships guarantee you a new opportunity, but relationships can help your credentials to be considered the next time a chance for promotion is available.

Step Three: Don't Stay on the Sidelines but Demonstrate New Skills

Become an active participant in any new group. When starting out, it is always a sound idea to get a baseline understanding of the project and understand who the critical "players" are. Ultimately, you need to become action-oriented. Take on a small specific project for the new group that might demonstrate your ability to handle a budget, lead people, and manage programs. These are the skills you will need to move upward in any organization.

In your performance evaluations, discuss your new accomplishments and prove value to the organization by linking these to their mission and objectives. You must be able to point out, in a positive but not overly aggressive way, that your work has contributed to the organization's success by... and give specific examples to support your idea.

Let me stress here that there is a difference between lobbying assertively and lobbying to the point that others see you as too aggressive and self-absorbed. There is always an "art" to marketing. Self-promotion is a teachable skill, but must be practiced expertly so that your listener and audience receive the message and are not impacted negatively.

Step Four: Model Behaviors of the People Who Have the Position You Aspire to Obtain

This advice assumes you have keen powers of observation and can internalize some of the role model's characteristics. It is relatively easy to understand that you must dress the part at work or you should dress as if you're already in the next role level. For example, teachers who want to become principals may wear a jacket to work and dress differently than those who are strictly oriented to the student audience in a classroom.

The more difficult personal characteristics to emulate, however, are those that are integral to functioning successfully in the next role level. Here's a simplistic example—get to work early and stay late. As you begin to work extra hours, beyond the normal hours of the position's general requirement and without expectation of additional compensation, you will be noticed.

Usually it is less about the time spent on the job and more about the characteristics you bring to the job. This might mean listening more rather than talking first in meetings or valuing everyone's opinion as much as your own. It is important for you to understand what your organization values. Watch who is promoted at the organization and why, and then you should model these behaviors to be noticed.

Step Five: Be Able to Negotiate a New Role and Salary for Yourself

Once you get a chance to advance your career with your current employer, you need to utilize a negotiation strategy related to a new title, salary, and responsibilities. As unlikely as it may seem, many women are undervalued because they do not try to negotiate. Whether you get what you request or not, the point is to exhibit behaviors valued by employers if you do negotiate. First and foremost in negotiating, demonstrate that you value yourself. Know your worth, and believe you are able to make a significant contribution.

In negotiations, you need strategy to guide the conversation, but many don't know how to begin. Here are several basic ideas to integrate into your thinking:

- The time to negotiate is when the offer for a new role is on the table and before you accept the position. Timing is everything.
- Do not ask about salary in an initial conversation, instead know the salary others make in similar positions before you get to the job offer stage.
- Begin by expressing delight in the offer and explain why you think this opportunity is such a good fit for your background and skills. You must project sincerity; I always suggest you indicate how important the new role

or promotion is to you. Ask for some time to consider the option, since the decision is so important for you and the organization.

- During this time out period, whether it is overnight or a few hours, you need to think about what, if anything, you want to negotiate concerning the offer. Do you want a higher salary, additional staff, and flexibility in work hours, or a travel and expense budget?

- When you reconnect with the employer, reemphasize the fit between your skills and the job responsibilities. Next, say you are interested in exploring other possibilities the organization may consider with regard to (increased salary, flexibility, etc.)

All the organization can really say is "no" to a negotiation request. You need to know immediately if you will, or will not, accept the role if they cannot compromise on your request. There are elements of skill in these negotiation conversations that tap into your interpersonal communication style. Remember, you will never know if you don't ask. The problem I have seen is that many women don't ask and as a result leave money on the table.

LOYALTY, PATIENCE, AND POLITICAL SAAVY REWARDED

All of us know a woman like this…Taylor went to work after her children were born to supplement the income of her husband, a high school science teacher. She was very good at what she did—received excellent evaluations from her supervisors, and developed a reputation at her organization as someone with detail orientation, excellent interpersonal and team skills, and follow through on all assignments.

After her first few years on the job, Taylor was ready for a new challenge but was not in a position financially to return to school or to move to another location. Taylor and I talked about how she could move forward within her organization, and I suggested additional education. We discussed the pros and cons of this because her income was critical to the family's financial health, and she was actively involved in her children's upbringing. After she decided she could not return to school, we talked again and she laughed when she said her main goal was to, "keep her head down, do a good job, and stay out of the politics in the work environment." What she said in jest became the mantra of her work.

A few years later, Taylor was asked to take on a new role, and again she demonstrated the same consistent performance. True to herself, she did not participate in any of the "negative talk" that often occurs in a work situation; she stayed focused on things she could control in her own work environment. Now 15 years later, this woman has had four different assignments within the organization, each one bringing her new perspective, new skills, and increased compensation.

Her inability to move to seek new challenges and a new salary level was compensated by increased seniority and years of service to the organization, as well as her ability to ask for additional responsibilities and negotiate several in-grade promotions. Taylor has been promoted while staying in place.

Today, marketing ourselves is critical for everyone because we live in a society that requires us to all become independent contractors and to take responsibility for our own promotion and upward mobility. With no guarantees of lifelong employment, loyalty to employees is sacrificed for the bottom line in many businesses. It is up to each of us to manage our own careers as life changes and progresses.

CHAPTER TEN

Don't Be Afraid of Conflict at Work

The Tenth Career Principle Is to Learn How to Address Work Conflicts

The tenth principle is somewhat counter-intuitive to all the others that were previously discussed. I have talked about how important it is to understand yourself and your motives. It is important to become intentional and take ownership for your working life as you develop a career. It is also very important to be authentic and true to your own self. This chapter is about the importance of relationships with others: how important it is to maintain some emotional distance at work, and not let your ego and self-esteem get too involved in workplace conflicts. It is about finding balance at work.

Success with this principle begins by accepting that conflict is an inevitable part of the human condition. In fact, a study reported in the *Leadership Quarterly* in 1996[1] found that 42 percent of a manager's time at work is on reaching agreement when conflicts occur. Conflict occurs frequently whenever there are different goals, work styles, and personality types. We all know the stories.

It is critical to have the sophistication and emotional maturity to strike the balance between ownership of your job and passion about your work, while also focusing on the completion of a project even when there are conflicts. Ultimately, we have to get the job done!

Successful women, who have obtained leadership positions and managed others, tell me they have learned conflict at work must not be viewed as a personal attack. It does not affect their self-esteem. Many women, however, do not handle conflict well and try to avoid it whenever possible. This can lead to quiet anger, avoiding confrontation at any cost to them, and not resolving interpersonal issues when necessary.

Why is this? Educational researchers tell us that female children focus on the importance of relationships as they begin to play in groups. Research in the field of career development also explains that as we mature, women focus effort on the development of a lifetime of different roles as mother, friend, employee, daughter, and spouse. These roles all involve the development of relationships with others. It then follows, that many women do give importance to developing relationships at work and at times, the job does become too personal.

_____

GAIL'S STORY

One woman I recently assisted had just resigned her position in upper management because of a difference of opinion with the governing board of her college. Early in our conversation, Gail expressed pain and hurt because if she did not resign, she realized her long-term employer would probably fire her. Always a positive employee, she had received superb evaluations and was recognized as a strong team player. She felt sad at this turn of events and the changes that were coming to her work environment. She expressed strong feelings of loyalty to the school and its students and looked for a change or compromise but there was none. She was angry and conflicted about her impending decision to resign.

In this case, no compromise would end her personal conflict. The only way Gail could find a win or a positive was to step away from the conflict, because she made a decision about the kind of organization she wanted to support. Just two weeks after her resignation, we talked about her exit strategy. She was able to begin articulating her feelings and think about her future plans. Her time of conflict and emotional turmoil was behind her. Gail understood she had made a career choice that enabled her to stay true to a personal value system.

Once she accepted that the conflict and resulting stress had been part of a systemic change at the institution, Gail understood that the conflict was not personal. She knew her resignation was not performance related. Only after thinking this through and putting some distance between herself and the job, could this woman began to radiate enthusiasm for a new beginning. What started out as a negative conflict ultimately became a way for this woman to find an even better work environment for herself. After her resignation, this woman examined in detail what had caused her conflict with the governing board so she knew what to look for in any new situations.

We talked about how the new leadership at her former organization had brought in a new vision and new goals. The new vision was not one she shared, and once this became clear, the stage had been set for the change. After de-personalizing the change and resulting conflict with the Board of Trustees and president, this very capable woman leader moved forward. Her next job search focused on her geographic preferences. She found a new challenging environment at a larger organization that fit her value system for student development and educational goals.

For many women, however, it is impossible to resign or leave to find a new job. The ability to find compromise with conflicts at work when you cannot resign is another critical skill to develop. In the oriental culture, they say it is important to help others keep their honor and save "face," and finding a compromise during a workplace conflict is a similar notion. Everyone has to step away from the conflict feeling as if he or she is still valued as an employee and not lost the respect of others.

Conflict relates to the ability to communicate. Perhaps someone didn't finish their part of the project, and you had to complete the assignment on your own, but still share the rewards or grade. Did you communicate your viewpoint effectively to your teammate? On the other hand, did conflict operate in your work environment because there was someone you just could not get along with no matter the circumstance? Were you using a different communication style than your co-worker?

Because conflict and difference of opinions are part of every work situation, the successful manager can resolve conflict. I refer people to the Steven Covey model of formulating "win-

win" propositions. He talks about this in his classic book, *The Seven Habits of Highly Effective People*.[2] As a manager, you will want to find ways so everyone walks away from the conflict a winner and saves face in some form. If that is not possible, then as Steven Covey suggests, you decide there is "no deal" and walk away from the incident or disagreement. You must have the ability to help people move on in the conflict.

Managing through conflict by using this model has to do with de-escalating the situation first. For example, it might involve the manager saying, "I understand you are angry." and acknowledging the legitimate feelings. Once the feelings are acknowledged, the manager must try to understand what the situation involves from all perspectives, and find a way to have everyone win and build the compromise in some way. In the conflict resolution model, the players can also decide they are not going to play in the game any longer. Bottom line—it is critical to use effective communication skills with all the parties involved, and realize that differences of opinion in the workplace do not have to become personal. It is not about you. It is about the work, so do not let it get too personal. This is a key—do not personalize conflict at work. Let me tell you another example of a way to find compromise.

SANDY'S CONFLICT BECAME A TEACHABLE MOMENT

Sandy was a young professional who ended up in tears at work one afternoon about ten years ago, and I came in to help resolve the argument. Today, Sandy is a successful team leader managing her own projects and employees, and recently told me how important that first experience with workplace conflict was to the success she has as a manager today. After the experience she learned how critical it is to confirm communications and directions; that she must take on issues as they are developing, rather than letting them escalate into full-blown arguments; and that conflicts can be resolved so each person ends up feeling valued and able to continue the job.

Sandy's conflict at work began with a personal miscommunication issue, but it also was about lack of space to concentrate when working on big projects. Two women were sharing a very tiny office space in a start-up organization, which was waiting a year for more appropriate quarters. Expectations were high as the organization wanted this group to develop a new product, and everyone was expecting great things from their collaboration. It was very tight working accommodations in a stressful environment. There was no privacy when using the telephone, both had difficulty concentrating, and there was very little room to spread out work. It was an impossible situation.

The conflict ignited due to poor communication. One woman misunderstood a deadline and the other woman gave unclear directions. In this case, the argument pointed out the complex and larger issues of personal space and privacy in office settings. The causes were transparent after the conflict, but not before the shouting began. One day loud shouts and crying came across the office suite and, when others opened the door on the team, both of the women sharing the office were angry, shouting at the same time, and one was in tears. Here was conflict in the workplace and a manager that had a project that had to be on time.

The manager immediately listened to both points of view with all parties in the room. Each side was reminded that they were both doing a good job. It was decided that no one needed to take the blame for this incident. There was acknowledgement that there were environmental causes with the space issues. Both agreed that, at times, even great communicators are misunderstood and/or can give unclear directions.

The manager and the two employees discussed how important it was to expedite the project and were asked to put aside the differences and move forward. One woman was given permission to work in another location, and both parties in this conflict let the other save face. No one was declared a winner and no one was declared a loser. They agreed they had disagreed and moved on for the sake of the project. Now, ten years later, when asked about that rocky afternoon, both women laugh and say it was a lesson learned. It was a conflict that had to be de-escalated immediately and it allowed both people to emerge to work together another day.

There are times when conflicts cannot be solved as easily as in these two examples. In certain situations, it is also important to know when to take a time out and leave the area to let the conflict end. If you know work should not become personal, it is possible to say you are sorry about the conflict and start again later when emotions have settled down. Try to use the time after a conflict to understand the other perspectives and causes of conflict. Develop a plan to turn what you have learned into a positive for yourself.

CHAPTER ELEVEN

It is Important to Always Strive for Balance

Final Thoughts

A full and satisfying life is not having to choose "all or nothing" nor must it be "either/or." Instead, a full life is about achieving balance in the various facets of your life. Contrary to the famous Mae West quote, "Too much of a good thing can be wonderful,"[1] in work too much of a good thing is not always good. Are you someone who: wakes up at night worrying about work; doesn't have enough time to take care of yourself; and feels guilty about not having time for your personal-life and community roles? Join the club! Many feel there are not enough hours in the day to take care of personal-life, work-life, and themselves.

Long work hours, over a sustained length of time, can become a problem even when you want to be on the "fast track" with your career, and you willingly compromise your personal-life to achieve success. In the United States culture, we have historically valued working longer hours that have contributed to our national productivity and great success. The standard workweek has varied from 35 hours during the Great Depression to an average of 47 hours per week during World War II, and even longer hours per week more recently. Globalization, competition, and consumerism have all contributed to our goals and our longer working hours. We work more hours than most European countries, and we are also the country that intimately understands the terms, workaholic and type 'A' personality.

Many of us grew up believing that hard work is a virtue. It still is. However, we know now that too much workload, too much multi-tasking, and too little control at work are all factors directly related to stressful work environments and in turn poor health. The costs are high for individuals, families, and employers dealing with stress-related illnesses. In fact, two websites, the American Institute on Stress,[2] and the Center for the Promotion of Health in the New England Workplace at the University of Massachusetts Lowell,[3] have many resources related to this topic.

According to Anne Perkins who reviewed a recent book by Harvard Medical School Associate Professor Herbert Benson, *The Relaxation Response*, in the *Harvard Business Review*, Benson's studies showed that stress reductions program decreased employees' visits to doctors by up to 50 percent. Benson also found that over 75 percent of physician visits are related to stress with a cost to industry over 200 billion dollars a year.[4]

Today, many more workplaces offer flexible work schedules, provide maternity benefits or family leave for elder care, and enable us to use technologies to work off-site and across geographic boundaries. This flexibility has helped us to achieve more balance between work and our personal lives. Many women have become entrepreneurs to gain control of work and time. Did you know that during the 1980s, employers and work place researchers began to see the public's priorities change to include the family's needs in employment or relocation decisions? College students graduating this year are definitely asking about benefit packages during job negotiations, and workplace family-friendly cultures are as important as salary to many young people.

Work and life balance do not have to be the Ying and Yang opposites of one another. Instead, I have found that women who claim they are successful and satisfied with life have discovered a way to create a fluid, almost permeable, boundary between the time and attention placed on work and the other parts of their lives. In finding that balance or equilibrium, they create life satisfaction. They talk about being happy with how they have spent their lives. Finding this satisfaction and balance is essential for most people.

So what is balance? Here are a few definitions:

Balance is a state of equilibrium where there is equality of distribution. It is the point where one weight balances or counter balances another weight. Balance is the harmonious arrangement of parts within a whole. As John Ruskin, a famous art critic said, "In all perfectly beautiful objects there is found the opposition of one part to another and a reciprocal balance."[5]

The need to find equality of distribution for our time and efforts directed towards work, life, and self is an eternal quest for women. But, what are we trying to balance? It has helped me to understand what we are balancing by visualizing our lives as three baskets that include our personal-life, work-life, and self-life.

I chose the basket icon because baskets were used in a variety of cultures for thousands of years; they are interwoven containers, most typically made of organic materials. For me, the interwoven basket represents the multiple threads and experiences of our lives. As I visualize these baskets, they represent where we put our efforts and time over the course of our lifetime. Each basket contains the roles we hold during our lives, and the projects and work that we complete in each of our life roles.

Our life baskets are very individualistic because they reflect how we divide our time and show how we focus and prioritize our life. We decide how much time to put into each basket based on what we value and carry with us from our culture. We change our emphasis, or how much time and attention we give to a particular basket, over the course of our lifetime because our needs and roles change.

It is important, when thinking about the baskets, to remember that you only have one life to live. You also have only 100 percent of your time to divide. Even though many of us operate at times as if we have more, no one really has 125 percent to give! There are, of course, certain moments in our lives we do have to pay our dues and put a higher percentage of effort into just one basket or area of life. However, over the course of a lifetime, no one should put everything into one basket if he or she is going to achieve balance and find overall life satisfaction.

The first basket of life that I visualize represents our personal-life. It includes the roles, time, and effort spent on others who are important to us. For example, it includes our time spent when we were children. It includes the time we spend as a student involved in education. It contains the relationships we have with friends, spouses, parents, and others in our community.

The second is our work-life basket. Included here are all of the things we intentionally expend effort to accomplish something important to us. This would include work we complete, in both paid and unpaid roles. Even your volunteer work becomes part of the career and work-life basket. In the work basket are accomplishments while employed, our ability to lead and manage projects, as well as supporting ourselves financially. We create and complete tasks in this basket.

The third basket is effort and time spent that involves us as an individual. It is the self-life basket. This represents the time and effort you devote to your own life, and might include health and fitness time, leisure pursuits, or your intellectual and spiritual life. This is a critical basket to utilize, as it must be filled sufficiently so you can effectively put efforts into your personal- and work-life. However, it is the third basket I have found most often receives the least amount of time and attention.

Here are elements that are critical to finding and achieving this balance in life:

- Know yourself—What is/will be truly important to you as you evaluate your life.
- Keep the focus on your life goals—Incorporate planning into your goals and stay true to them.
- Sustainability—You must expend effort and strength to reach the goals in your baskets, as life is a process, and success in a role does not happen quickly.
- Flexibility—Adapt the amount and degree of effort you

put into the baskets as life moves forward with changes in circumstance, both internal and external, as these come from the world and people around you.

- Revitalize—Update and/or recycle when the balance shifts. Nothing stays the same and, at times, the baskets may get out of balance without your realization.

It is important to communicate the values accurately that guide your efforts in the three baskets to others who are important in your life. It is also important for you to become intentional about achieving balance and how you are dividing and focusing your time. To assist you, I've listed questions to think about:

- If 100 percent is all you can give to all three baskets of roles, how much are you giving to each of your baskets today?
- What are the roles, people, or projects in your baskets of work/personal/self?
- How have the roles in your baskets changed over time due to circumstance?
- How do you know when you are overloading one of the baskets?
- How can you shift the weights (time/efforts/number of projects) put into the baskets?
- How will the amount of effort you can expend on the roles in the baskets change as you age?

Losing your balance can begin with an imperceptive shift and the addition of just one more project that needs more time to get accomplished. Usually, the addition of one project is not going to throw off the balance of the three baskets, unless it is an extremely large and time-consuming new responsibility. Balance tends to change with an accumulative effect.

―――――――――

Here are some real life examples from women who suddenly realized, without noticing, the balance had shifted with the distribution of their efforts. The balance of the baskets had changed dramatically. Can you see yourself in any of these descriptions?

IT WASN'T JUST ONE NEW PROJECT THAT PUT WORK OUT OF BALANCE

One day Carolyn woke up and realized work's percentage of time and effort had changed without her even knowing when the weight of the work basket began to shift. Does this sound like you? At work, Carolyn had a twenty-five-year career with the same organization; she had earned two degrees while she was on the staff. After completing the second degree, Carolyn sought out a new role and was asked to take on new projects and assignments. As she could be counted on to do a good job, she got the promotion.

At first, she began to stay a little late and worked from home on the weekends to get the job done. She gave up vacation days to meet the increasing demands. Finally, she was asked to take on a second, completely new job responsibility, because a teammate could not be replaced in the bad economy in a workplace with declining revenues. There was no money to hire a replacement when a resignation occurred. Carolyn was now doing two jobs for the same salary.

Slowly the balance had shifted. What began with Carolyn looking for new responsibilities, to keep her intellectually involved, became way out of balance for her. It was not one project that threw her basket out of balance, but an accumulation of small things that eventually become too much to carry. Her work-life had thrown her personal-life and self-life out of balance.

LEE'S PERSONAL-LIFE BASKET BECAME TOO HEAVY CARING FOR AN AGING PARENT

Lee's personal-life basket weight began to change when she agreed to take care of an aging parent. The new responsibility was taken with love and, at first, was compartmentalized to one day a weekend, a few occasional hours during the week, and some new tasks. Then her parent experienced a medical emergency, and Lee found herself spending all of her time and effort outside of work concentrating on her personal-life basket.

She found more time to carry the heavier personal-life basket by giving the self-basket less time and less attention. She stopped doing the things that had kept her healthy. Daily exercise disappeared and all meals were fast food grabbed on the way to or from the nursing home. Eventually Lee began to have her own medical problems that forced her to miss work. All three baskets were now out of balance because Lee could not meet the obligations of a heavy personal-life basket. The weights had shifted dramatically.

WHAT STARTED OUT AS HEALTHY EXERCISE BECAME AN OBSESSION

Diane was an exercise physiologist and taught at a private college in the Midwest about ten years ago. Because she was such a strong advocate for health and wellness, she was able to have an exercise component added to the requirements for each student who graduated. At the same time, Diane began to jog before coming to campus every day to live the personal-life style she taught and asked others to achieve. Her basket focused on self-care; her work- and personal-life baskets were all well balanced.

Several years later, Diane began to train for marathons, which meant an increased training regimen that became a long run in the morning before work and one after work. Before long Diane was also running over the noon hour and her department chair and others began to complain. Diane's office hours were nonexistent and she was unavailable to her students. What started out as a wonderful way of living her goal of health and fitness became too heavy for the self-basket and her work and career suffered.

Another area of balance that is important to many women is the dual career pattern. Many have asked, "How can you find the balance between the needs of your personal-life, your work-life, and self-life when you are part of a dual career couple, especially when each of the partners is fully engaged in professional development and the income is needed to reach their goals?"

Here are some strategies to consider which other dual career couples found worked for their mutual success:

- Prioritizing one career for a time—"Your career will lead first." The career of one partner has priority to begin, and then after a period of time and certain degree of success, the second career takes over the lead and priority in decisions about relocation, etc.
- Alternating the lead in the decision-making—"Let's take turns when we must make a decision that impacts both of our careers." The individual's career needs are considered at each promotion or relocation decision point, and they alternate the lead in the decision. Both of the careers are moving forward in tandem.

WHEN BOTH PARTNERS ARE WORKING

One of my former clients was highly successful in her field. The person was promoted quickly through the entry-level positions and was a rising star known to many in national organizations. However, things began to go wrong with her life plans when she accepted a work position in another state before consulting the family. Two years later, she was a vice president as she had planned, but her marriage had ended in divorce and her children were living in a shared custody arrangement. Life and work goals had collided and there was no compromise. Her trailing spouse was forced into a relocation of work as well, and the move to a new geographic location was one that neither the husband nor children had embraced.

Years later, Myra began to work with me. In a succession of other positions, Myra achieved a certain degree of success, but as she approached her retirement planning, she looked back with regret. As she talked about her life and career, she realized this particular career decision was not built on work and life balance. It had been a pivotal life-changing decision that had long-term ramifications both financially and emotionally. She was approaching retirement with less money and less enthusiasm for the next steps in life than others she knew. Myra was unclear about how to move forward without her career as the main driving force of her life. Her personal-life and self-needs had been denied equality with that of her work-life.

Myra's choice illustrates that both women and men can let work and life roles become unbalanced. Let's talk about a different approach—one that has turned out more positive.

ANOTHER EXAMPLE OF A DUAL CAREER PARTNERSHIP

Both John and his wife have enjoyed their work lives and experienced career success. This couple met in graduate school and when they married, they agreed that the wife's career would lead in any re-location necessary for upward mobility, and that the man would develop a portable career that would be more entrepreneurially based. Part of their planning also included not having children. They moved several times and each time the wife led the transition. She sought the promotion and relocation, while the husband continued to build his career as a writer. This type of arrangement appears more frequently now in two career couples.

VARIATION ON THE THEME

Another variation is for one career to lead for a period and then for the other partner's career to lead at the next relocation opportunity. These patterns show an awareness of the importance of work and life balance as a factor in career success.

For one couple, the husband was an attorney in the military and his career lead the first 20 years until his retirement. While his career led, the wife cared for the children and attended graduate school. After the husband's retirement, they decided that the wife's career would begin to lead and he would practice law as a consultant wherever she needed them to relocate. Ultimately, the wife became one of the first women chief operating officers at a large organization where she was recognized for outstanding leadership. She spoke to other women about the time when she had been the "stay at home" mom. Her mentoring of other women with leadership potential was well known in the field.

CONCLUSION

In summary, the demands of our lives do change, as we have seen in the examples above. There will be times that you must change the amount of time and emphasis you give to your work basket because your other roles in life shift. This is why I suggest you visualize work and life balance as fluid.

I hope the notes for success shared in the preceding chapters will help you become all that you can be and all that you visualize for yourself. Your career and life satisfaction are closely interwoven and interdependent. Understanding that your life is a journey that involves finding the balance between all of life's roles is important. Take care of yourself and enjoy both work and life. Best of luck!

ACHIEVE IT!

APPENDIX A

INTRODUCTION TO WORKSHEETS

Decision-making and evaluation of the next career steps become easier by writing down your thoughts, career options, and goals. The exercises included in *VOICES — Words from Wise Women* were developed around the sound career theories of Frank Parsons, Donald Duper, John Holland, and others. People who understand themselves and have an accurate picture of the contemporary economy and work environment, will be able to find a satisfying job and subsequent career.

The first set of exercises will help you tap into your life roles—the time and value you attach to each of your roles. You will identify your strengths/weaknesses, be able to speak about these to others, and factor them into any decision-making. Finally, you will identify your life and work goals and values.

Ideally, you should plan to use these exercises every two to three years. As we know, adult needs and interests continue to develop throughout a lifetime. What may be right for you now may not be a good fit for you in the future. Every time you begin a career transition, take the time to do a self-assessment. It will help you develop your goal(s), assist in building a targeted job search, and ensure you will be satisfied with the fit of your next job and career step.

Directions: Conduct a thorough self-assessment by responding to the questions in the following exercises.
- Give thoughtful consideration to your answers, as they will become the basis on which you will make further career decisions.
- Do not answer to meet societal or familial expectations but rather to bring your authentic personal considerations forward for planning purposes.

Goals: To understand:
- Your roles
- Needs
- Skills/abilities
- Interests/values
- Social considerations or parameters that will shape your preference for particular work

Outcome: The key ingredient of successful career management is accurate self-assessment.
- You must understand who you are and what you want, before you can get there!
- You will be exploring your personal history and individual characteristics to make yourself both marketable in any future job searches and/or to achieve your personal goals.

APPENDIX B

WHO ARE YOU?

Directions:

- Explore the roles you hold in life and how important each is to you. For example, are you a mother? Are you a volunteer for an organization? Are you a student?
- List the roles in which you expend effort at this point in your life.
- For each role, attach a weight to illustrate how much time you spend in this role, and a second weight to how much importance you attach to this role.
- Use a numbering system from 1 to 10 for the weighting, with 10 the most important and 1 to indicate your least important role.
- Use the same system to create a second score that would indicate your most time-consuming role. A 10 would be most time-consuming, while 1 would be the least time consuming.

ROLES   **RATING**

I am a_____ Importance_____ Time Spent_____

I am a_____ Importance_____ Time Spent_____

I am a_____ Importance_____ Time Spent_____

I am a_____ Importance_____ Time Spent_____

Now look at the roles and note which roles have the highest numerical values. At this time in your life, what are the roles that exert the most influence, based on importance and time? These roles must be factored into your career decision-making and development for the next few years. List the items that must be balanced within your career.

Role No. 1

_____

_____

_____

_____

_____

_____

_____

Role No. 2

_____

_____

_____

_____

_____

_____

Role No. 3

_____

_____

_____

_____

_____

_____

APPENDIX C

WHAT ARE YOUR STRENGTHS IN WORK AND LIFE?

Directions:

- Create a list of both your strengths and weaknesses. Try to be as honest and objective as you can.
- Once you have created the list, review the list with a colleague, spouse, or other person with whom you are close and knows you well.
- The second opinion will expand your thinking about yourself. For example, they may suggest a strength or weakness that you did not consider for this list.
- It will also confirm the elements of your personal assessment and validate the answers you have developed.
- Use keywords to capture these thoughts.

Strengths:

1. _____

_____

2. _____

_____

3. _____

_____

4. _____

_____

5. _____

_____

Challenges / Weaknesses:

1. _____

_____

2. _____

_____

3. _____

_____

4. _____

_____

5. _____

_____

Analysis for Future Decision-Making:

What are the two key strengths you want to emphasize?

_____

_____

_____

_____

_____

_____

_____

_____

What are the areas of challenge you would like to avoid?

_____

_____

_____

_____

_____

_____

APPENDIX D

WHAT ARE YOUR GOALS IN LIFE?

Directions:

- The following list is not by any means complete, but it will provide an opportunity to attach a priority to some of your goals. Please feel free to add other items that may be critical to you.
- Complete this assessment quickly without long deliberation. These goals are very broad and may be values.
- Rank the 18 goals in order, from the most important to the least important. Use the number 1 for your most important goal, and the number 18 for the least important goal.

( ) Wealth — earn a great deal of money
( ) Service — contribute to the satisfaction of others
( ) Leadership — become influential and lead other people
( ) Pleasure — enjoy life—to be happy and content
( ) Independence — have freedom of thought and action
( ) Expertise — become an authority
( ) Acceptance — be received with approval
( ) Parenthood — raise a fine family—have heirs
( ) Self-Realization — optimize personal development
( ) Security — have a secure and stable position
( ) Prestige — become well known and have status
( ) Stability — have the ability or strength to withstand change
( ) Duty — dedicate to responsibility
( ) Recognition — receive acknowledgment or commendation
( ) Affection — obtain and share companionship and affection
( ) Professionalism — attain work goals
( ) Intimacy — be close to others
( ) Power — have control of others

- List your top five goals below and plan to keep them in mind daily. Some people list these in a planner or keep them on their desks.

1. _____

_____

2. _____

_____

3. _____

_____

4. _____

_____

5. _____

_____

APPENDIX E

WHAT ARE YOUR WORK GOALS?

Directions:

- Check the items below that you would like to incorporate in a work situation.
- What kind of job would you want?

    ( ) Supervisory

    ( ) Decision-making

    ( ) Creative

    ( ) Math-oriented

    ( ) People-oriented

    ( ) Physically challenging

    ( ) Mentally stimulating

    ( ) Easy to do

    ( ) Filled with responsibility

    ( ) Mechanical

- How much money do you want to make?

    ( ) Enough to make a real effort essential

    ( ) Enough to meet bills comfortably

    ( ) Enough on which to get rich

    ( ) Enough for minimum requirements

- What fringe benefits do you want?

    ( ) Medical and life insurance

    ( ) Good retirement

    ( ) Stock options

    ( ) Part ownership possibilities

    ( ) Country club and other social benefits

    ( ) Company car

- What self-satisfaction do you need?

    ( ) Creative urge satisfaction

    ( ) Pride in doing something socially useful

    ( ) A sense of overcoming challenges

    ( ) A feeling of growth

- Where does your future lie?

    ( ) In building experience for future growth

    ( ) In accepting more and more responsibility

APPENDIX F

PERSONAL AND CAREER HISTORY

Directions:

We are naturally influenced by the sum of our experience. Our view of the world is shaped by a personal background including family patterns, world view, and life messages we receive and learn from our unique cultural backgrounds and life experiences. These play out in the careers we choose for ourselves, our expectations for the future, and our definitions of success and failure.

Take some time to fill out the personal and work history below and analyze what importance they may have on your decisions and career planning.

NAME: _____

AGE: _____

MARITAL STATUS: _____

• List the members and occupations of your present family and your family of origin. If the person is deceased, identify their education and occupations when living.

	NAME	AGE	EDUCATION	OCCUPATION
FATHER:				
MOTHER:				

BROTHERS: _____
_____
_____

SISTERS: _____
_____
_____

SPOUSE: _____
_____
_____

CHILDREN: _____
_____
_____

- Describe your education and training including the highest grade you completed in school.

_____
_____
_____

- Describe your occupation.

_____
_____
_____

- What is the present state of your health? Identify any health problems.

_____
_____
_____

Employment History:

- Account for all of your time during the past ten years including any military service, periods of unemployment, starting with your current position and working backwards through time.

CURRENT POSITION   DATES OF EMPLOYMENT   TITLE   DUTIES

1. _____

_____

_____

2. _____

_____

_____

3. _____

_____

_____

4. _____

_____

_____

5. _____

_____

_____

Development Work History:

Describe memories of your father's work.

Describe memories of your mother's work.

How did your parents feel about their work?

Do you have the same work attitudes and behaviors as your parents?

When you were a child was there anyone whose job interested or impressed you? Why?

Did you ever think of doing that work yourself? Why or why not?

Describe early experiences of work that stand out in your memory.

Did anyone in your childhood expect or want you to do a certain job when you grew up?

What were your family's values with reference to work? (For example, always do your best.)

APPENDIX G

How Does the Economy Impact Your Work?

Directions:

This activity will assist in a review of the state of the economy and its impact on your job function and industry segment. As you consider these questions make some brief notes to yourself. Your answers will be used to guide your consideration of available career options.

1. Are you bound by any geographic considerations that might limit your career options?

2. Is there a time line associated with these geographic concerns or limitations?

3. What are the current trends in your industry or work that are factors in hiring and promotion practices?

4. How do these trends factor into your geographic target zone?

5. Who are the key players in your industry?

6. Who are the key players in your industry within your geographic target zone?

7. Are there some established networking colleagues who you should contact to help think through a career decision or transition?

8. How would you evaluate your chance of making a successful transition, at this moment, on a scale of 1-10 with 10 being the highest degree of success?

9. What would happen to your current role if you chose not to make a career decision or transition at this time?

APPENDIX H

DESCRIBE YOUR IDEAL JOB AND CREATE A VISION FOR YOUR FUTURE

Directions:

Consider the possibilities. Find a quiet place where you can relax. Close your eyes and imagine yourself one year from now at work. It is morning and you get up for work, get dressed, and drive to the office. Now breathe life into the scenario for yourself. Use the following ideas and space to stimulate your thinking. Your goal is to create a vision of yourself at this work.

Position title:

Industry or type of organization:

Scope of your responsibilities:

Geographic location:

Corporate culture or environment:

Skills you will use:

Salary level:

- What will your supervisor be like?

- What will the people you work with be like?

- How does this job fit into your broad life goals?

- Is there work and life balance?

- Are there other considerations?

APPENDIX I

DEVELOP A PRELIMINARY BUSINESS PLAN FOR YOURSELF

This is something we do for others but rarely for ourselves. Take some time to think about setting goals for yourself and the steps it will take to implement your goals.

Directions:

Please develop your career options based on your answers to the previous appendices you have already completed.

Career Option One:

Career Option Two:

Career Option Three:

- What research do you need to complete before one of the options is implemented?

- What issues will need to be resolved before you can begin to implement the plan?

- List people you should talk with to gain information and insight before you begin the plan:

Name:

Name:

Name:

- What additional certifications, training, or education will you need to complete?

- What time line can you develop for yourself to set this action plan in place?

- What decision-making method will you use to select your next career option?

- What priorities will guide your decision-making?

APPENDIX J

ANALYZE SOME SPECIFIC JOB POSSIBILITIES

Find at least three specific job advertisements that appeal to you by using postings for employment either that appear online, in newspapers, or in professional publications related to your area of interest. Be sure to note job qualifications described in the advertisement and salary information.

Directions:

Use the format below to consider the possibilities for each job posting. Compare the position with your skills, values, and needs. Look for those that are a good fit and analyze which jobs do not meet the criteria you have set in the series of activities you have previously completed.

Job Posting No. 1 — Title:

POSITION REQUIREMENTS	YOUR STRENGTHS	YOUR GAPS/WEAKNESSES
Experience		
Credentials		
Characteristics		
Quality of life considerations		
Salary posted		

APPENDIX K

REWORK YOUR RESUME

It is important to update your credentials annually. Your professional summary and accomplishment statements are the most critical sections of the resume.

Use this activity to write the summary. Everything else on your document will prove what you have said in this section.

Directions:

To develop the "Professional Summary" section of your resume, follow these suggestions:

- Ideas to capture include your experience, areas of expertise, skills, personal characteristics, and anything else that makes you unique.
- You can write them either as four to five bullets that are incomplete sentences, or several lines of text followed by several bullets.
- Get started by writing five keywords for each of the topics you need to include and highlight in the professional summary section.
- Then construct these into concise statements that market your accomplishments to the reader.

Write five keywords that describe you for each of the topics below. These will enable the resume reader to understand your overall career goals and previous achievements.

Previous title and experience _____

_____

Areas of expertise _____

_____

Skills _____

_____

Personal characteristics or other unique qualities _____

_____

A few professional summary statements are shown below to help get your thinking started:

Sample One:
- Senior-level communications executive with 20 years of high visibility in Washington, DC
- Best-selling author and crisis management expert in government, media, communications, and public relations
- Top level speech writer/resources and economic development management
- Association management executive for trade associations

Sample Two:
- Retail coordinator in exclusive designer- and apparel-related environments
- Sales, new business development, special events coordination
- Four years of high visibility positions in conjunction with major high-end retailers and specialty stores
- Recognized for enhancing sales 56% each season for past four years

Sample Three:
    A market-driven senior executive with outstanding qualifications in directing multimillion-dollar operations in global theaters. Recognized for capitalizing on existing product potential and identifying new growth opportunities.
- Visionary leadership/innovations management
- Production and efficiency optimization
- Customer service and retention management
- Business development and expansion

Now write your summary statements.

_____

_____

_____

_____

_____

Writing Accomplishment Statements on the Resume

After reading the Professional Summary section, employers will look for the accomplishments you have achieved at work. Use this quick system to think about and develop accomplishment statements.

What problem have you faced at work?

What are the actions you took?

What were the results achieved?

Remember your reader will be looking for you to quantify items and be action-oriented in every experience. Try to write at least two accomplishment statements for every employment entry.

1. PROBLEMS

ACTIONS

RESULTS

2. PROBLEMS

ACTIONS

RESULTS

3. PROBLEMS

ACTIONS

RESULTS

APPENDIX L

How to Develop a Negotiation Strategy

The time to negotiate for additional salary or other essential elements is between receiving the offer and accepting it. Use the activity below, to plan what items you will want to negotiate.

Directions:

Items to negotiate may include salary, relocation assistance, performance incentives, travel and expenses, continuing education support, health and retirement benefits, vacation, flexibility, mobile office support, and others.

Once you have received an offer, thank the employer and ask for time to make your decision. In this time out phase:

- Prioritize these lists and assign them a value on a scale of 1 to 5. Use 5 for the item that is most important.

What elements in this employment option are a good fit for you?

Items of fit include:

1.

2.

3.

4.

5.

What areas need to be addressed by the organization to close the deal?

Items to be negotiated include:

1.

2.

3.

4.

5.

APPENDIX M

EXPLORE YOUR BASKETS OF LIFE

This activity is helpful to understand how you are currently dividing your time between the three baskets discussed in this book. Each basket illustration shown below represents an area of your life.

Directions:

Assign the percentage of time you give to your *personal-life basket, your work-life basket, and your self-life basket.* Within each basket, write the roles and projects that occupy your time.

This activity will help you answer questions about life balance as well as clarify any changes you may want to make.

Questions to answer with this activity are:
- How do you currently prioritize your time and effort in your three baskets?
- What roles have you put into each basket?
- What projects are you doing within each of your roles?
- Are there baskets that are fuller or heavier than others?
- Are there baskets that are more important to you at this time than at another time of your life?

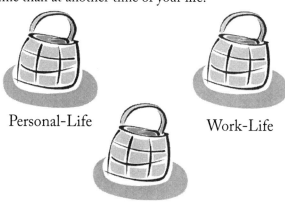

Personal-Life   Work-Life

Self-Life

Basket Activity

1.   Label each basket. I suggest you use a different color of ink for each.

2.   Assign a percentage of time to each basket representing the amount of time you devote to each of the baskets of life: work-life, personal-life, and self-life.

3.   On each of the circles write in the roles and projects you've assigned to each basket.

4.   Now observe what you have done with the baskets, remembering that each of us has only 100% of our time and effort to give to the combination of the three baskets.

5.   How much time have you assigned to each basket? Is one clearly larger or smaller than the other two baskets?

6.   Does one basket have more projects within it?

7.   At this moment of time in your life, is the assignment of your time and the number of projects you have put into each of the baskets both satisfying and appropriate?

8.   Why or why not is the balance a good fit for you now?

9.   What elements could you change?

Notes

Introduction
1. Mark D. Sanders and Tia Sillers, *I Hope You Dance* Lyrics, March 2003, Songwriters: available online at http://www.elyrics.net

Chapter One
1. Edgar Schein, *Career Anchors: Discovering Your Real Values*, (San Francisco: Jossey-Bass/Pfeiffer, 1990)
2. Carl Jung, 1875 to 1961 Swiss Psychiatrist, Myer's Briggs Personality Typology, http://www.personalitypage.com/html/info.html
3. Bureau of Labor Statistics, http://www.bls.gov
4. *Occupational Outlook Handbook*, http://www.bls.gov/oco

Chapter Two
1. Margaret Thatcher, Wikipedia Information, http://en.wikipedia.org/wiki/Margaret_Thatcher
2. Sally Fields, (1985 Academy Award) *Places in the Heart*, http://www.imdb.com/title/tt0087921/trivia

Chapter Three
1. Plato, Classical Greek philosopher and student of Socrates, (423BC to 348BC) Brainy Quote, http://www.brainyquote.com/quotes/authors/p/plato_3.html
2. Richard W. Judy and Carol D'Amico, *Workforce 2020, Work and Workers in the 21st Century*, (Indianapolis, Indiana: Hudson Institute, 1999)
3. U.S. Department of Education Statistics, http://nces.ed.gov/fastfacts
4. U.S. Department of Labor, http://www.dol.gov

Chapter Four
1. Charles Darwin, English Naturalist, February 1809 to April 1881, http://thinkexist.com/quotes/Charles_Darwin/
2. William Bridges, *Transitions: Making Sense of Life's Changes*, (New York, NY: Perseus Books Publishing, LLC, 1980)

Chapter Five
1. U.S. Department of Labor, *Occupational Outlook Handbook*, http://www.bls.gov

Chapter Six
1. Ronald E. Riggio, PhD, "Cutting-Edge Leadership," *Psychology Today*, Blog, March 18, 2009, http://www.psychologytoday.com/blog/cutting-edge-leadership
2. U.S. Department of Labor, Report on Glass Ceiling, http://www.mith2.umd.edu/WomensStudies/GenderIssues/GlassCeiling/LaborDeptInfo/glass-ceiling-initiative

Chapter Seven
1. Homer, *The Odyssey*, 800 B.C., Translated by Samuel Butler, http://classics.mit.edu/Homer/odyssey.mb.txt
2. American Chemical Society, *Women in the workplace: mentoring and flexibility are keys to advancement*, Science Blog, (April 2002), http://scienceblog.com/community/older/2002/D/2002409.html
3. Dick Gregory, "Hearts and Minds," http://heartsandminds.org/quotes/fulfill.htm
4. Norman Vincent Peale, Minister, Author, May 31, 1898 to December 24, 1993, http://www.brainyquote.com/quotes/authors/n/norman_vincent_peale_2.html

Chapter Eight
1. Charles Dubois, Belgian Naturalist, May 1804 to November 1867, Wikipedia, http://en.wikipedia.org/wiki/Charles_Fr%C3%A9d%C3%A9ric_Dubois

Chapter Nine
1. Charles Knight, http://www.museumkarketingtips.com
2. Tom Peters, (August 31, 1997) "Brand Called You," *Fast Company Magazine*, http://www.fastcompany.com/magazine/10/brandyou.html

Chapter Ten
1. C. Watson and R. Hoffman, "Managers as Negotiators," *Leadership Quarterly* 7 (1) (1996)
2. Stephen R. Covey, *The Seven Habits of Highly Effective People*, (New York, NY: Simon & Schuster, 1989)

Chapter Eleven

1. Mae West, American Actress, August 17, 1893 to November 22, 1980, http://www.brainyquote.com/quotes/quotes/m/maewest141679.html

2. American Institute of Stress, http://www.stress.org/

3. University of Massachusetts Lowell, http://www.uml.edu/centers/cph-new/job-stress/financial-costs.html

4. A. Perkins, "Saving Money by Reducing Stress," *Harvard Business Review* 72 (6): (1994), http://www.stress.org/job

5. John Ruskin, February 8, 1819 to January 20, 1900, English art critic and social thinker, http://www.thefreedictionary.com/proportion

About the Author

Dr. Kathy Jordan is a career transition specialist, a veteran employment expert, and pioneer of online human resource solutions. Well known for her work as an executive coach and advocate for women, she made numerous presentations on these subjects. Kathy's previous clients now hold top positions in Fortune 100 companies, higher education, government, and the not-for-profit sector. In addition to her consulting work, for the past ten years she was a director of Career Services in higher education helping thousands of young people each year. Before assuming this role, Kathy was the managing consultant for a leading provider of human resource services to corporations.

A graduate of the College of William and Mary with a degree in Sociology, Kathy also has a Masters in Counseling from Radford University and a Doctorate in Education and Counseling from Virginia Tech. Today, she is a Nationally Certified Career Counselor (NCCC) with over 20 years of experience in career counseling and coaching. She holds memberships in such professional organizations as the American Counseling Association and the National Association of Colleges and Employers.

She has been active in the business world as a member of the Board of Directors of the Chamber of Commerce, a member of the Society of Human Resource Managers, American Society for Training and Development, and as president of Main Street Radford, an economic development organization. As a graduate faculty member in higher education, she teaches students about the career counseling profession, has authored numerous articles and made presentations for national organizations. Dr. Jordan's specialties include executive-level career management and career transitions for women. She is a strong proponent of civic engagement and service to others and known for her accomplishments as a leader, team builder, and counselor.

Her professional philosophy includes working with clients to:

- Develop clarity of purpose and understanding self
- Understand contemporary work environments and identify and implement next career steps
- Build self-esteem and confidence in the job search process
- Integrate personal and career goals to develop a pro-active career management strategy

Dr. Jordan resides in Radford, Virginia, with her husband, a college professor. She and her husband have four grown daughters. For more information, visit her website at The Success Associates, www.thesuccessassociates.com

CPSIA information can be obtained at www.ICGtesting.com
Printed in the USA
BVOW030835081111

275559BV00002B/3/P